ALLEN PARK PUBLIC LIBRARY #4
8100 Allen Road
Allen Park, MI 48101-1708
313-381-2425

D0328522

GHOSTS, SPIRITS,
& HAUNTINGS

ALLEN PARK PUBLIC LIBRARY

133.1 P

Exposed, Uncovered, and Declassified:

Ghosts, Spirits, & Hauntings

Am I Being Haunted?

Edited by Michael Pye & Kirsten Dalley

A division of
The Career Press, Inc.
Pompton Plains, NJ

Copyright © 2011 by Michael Pye and Kirsten Dalley

All rights reserved under the Pan-American and International Copyright Conventions. This book may not be reproduced, in whole or in part, in any form or by any means electronic or mechanical, including photocopying, recording, or by any information storage and retrieval system now known or hereafter invented, without written permission from the publisher, The Career Press.

EXPOSED, UNCOVERED, AND DECLASSIFIED: GHOSTS, SPIRITS, & HAUNTINGS
EDITED BY KIRSTEN DALLEY
TYPESET BY DIANA GHAZZAWI
Cover design by Ian Shimkoviak/the BookDesigners
Printed in the U.S.A.

To order this title, please call toll-free 1-800-CAREER-1 (NJ and Canada: 201-848-0310) to order using VISA or MasterCard, or for further information on books from Career Press.

The Career Press, Inc.
220 West Parkway, Unit 12
Pompton Plains, NJ 07444
www.careerpress.com
www.newpagebooks.com

Library of Congress Cataloging-in-Publication Data
Available upon request.

Contents

ALLEN PARK PUBLIC LIBRARY #4
8100 Allen Road
Allen Park, MI 48101-1708
313-381-2425

9-0062 12054 8027

Preface

The subject of the afterlife and ghosts has a perennial appeal that transcends time and culture. After all, every single one of us will travel down that road eventually. Humanity has done its best to demystify what happens to us after death, thereby making it less frightening and perhaps even comforting (if indeed we end up in a better place). The ancient Egyptians gave food and sundries to their dead for their travels to the Otherworld; modern-day Mexico observes its *Dia de los Muertos* with a carnival-like atmosphere of drinking and parties; and Americans still enjoy trick-or-treating on Halloween, another ghostly holiday. But despite these varied and culturally sanctioned efforts to grapple with death and assimilate its grim inevitability into our consciousness, the doubts and fears linger. Death in any guise will always repulse us, and ghosts will always scare us.

Despite these fears, however, some people are drawn to the study of hauntings and ghosts. Some people actually *volunteer* to spend a night in a haunted house, chase ghosts, or contact the dead. For some, this is not just a job or a hobby, but an obsession. For years science has been reluctant to tackle the issues of ghostly phenomena and life after death, but during the last decade or so, a new openness to the paranormal has found purchase in the areas of scientific inquiry. Much of today's research is built upon the work that Dr. Raymond Moody started with his *Life After Life*. More recent scientific pioneers include John Lerma, MD, author of *Into the Light,* and Jeffrey Long , MD, author of *Evidence of the Afterlife,* both of whom have put their medical careers at risk by coming forward and telling people the truth about what they have witnessed. They do so not to gain fame or fortune, but because they can no longer ignore their deeply held belief that there is an afterlife and that the spirits of the dead are still trying to contact the living.

In this collection you will find a group of people on the front lines of inquiry into the paranormal, sharing their research and stories as only they can tell them. Follow them to ghostly climes as they chase poltergeists; come along to Gettysburg as they photograph long-dead Civil War soldiers; run alongside them as they chase down ghostly animals and cryptids; and observe them in psychiatric hospitals and the groves of academe and science as they seek out more prosaic explanations for paranormal activities and hauntings. But as you do so, remember what Nietzsche said— when you look into the abyss, the abyss also looks into you.

Are you ready?

—Kirsten Dalley and Michael Pye

August 2011

Haunted Houses:
Theaters of the Mind

By Andrew Nichols

Your house is your larger body. It grows in the sun and sleeps in the stillness of the night; and it is not dreamless.

—Kahlil Gibran, *The Prophet*

The image of the haunted house is firmly planted in our collective consciousness. In the ancient world it was a common belief that every dwelling had its own spirit, or *genius loci*, and it was honored and respected. Neglecting to make offerings to these guardian spirits of the home would almost certainly result in a run of bad luck, nightmares, or what we would today refer to as poltergeist activity. Most people today consider themselves too civilized to believe in fairies or goblins, but the belief in spirits of the dead and the archetypal haunted house is deeply rooted in the human psyche. The dark, decaying Victorian mansion, draped with cobwebs and probably adjacent to a crumbling cemetery; bats flying out of shattered windows; and shutters banging in the wind—these stereotypes, reinforced by Hollywood films and horror novels, actually have some basis in fact. It is true that older homes where generations have lived and died are more likely to be plagued by ghostly experiences than more modern structures, but most genuine haunted houses are far from fitting this image. Many newer homes, including those that have never been occupied, are believed to be haunted. I have even come across several haunted mobile homes and newly constructed apartment buildings. In some cases, a reputedly haunted structure is torn down, and another building constructed on the same site will continue to produce reports of ghostly phenomena. Although houses are the most commonly reported locations of hauntings (or haunts), there are also haunted churches, schools, businesses, apartment buildings, and stretches of road. Most haunts seem to be confined to a particular location, but some will follow the living inhabitants if they move to another location. Many hauntings also seem to be triggered by renovations or structural changes to a property.

A haunting or haunt may be defined as any location where certain types of paranormal experiences repeatedly occur. The most commonly reported phenomena are the sounds of footsteps or voices. These sounds may recur in one location within the house, such as the sound of footsteps on the stairs or down a particular hall. Sometimes these sounds occur at regular intervals, at certain times of night, or on certain days of the year. Another commonly reported phenomenon is the movement of objects or doors opening or closing by themselves. Cold spots may be experienced in the house. These spots may remain in one location or move around. Cold breezes may be felt, as if something invisible had passed by. Sometimes residents or visitors report the touch of unseen hands. Usually these touches are light and harmless, but punches, pushes, and bites are also occasionally reported. Apparitions are also frequently seen in haunted houses. These are the visible ghosts, and most often they resemble a living human being and appear to be completely solid. They are often mistaken for real living people until they vanish suddenly or walk through a wall or closed door. Apparitions may also be transparent or monochromatic. They may resemble a cloud of smoke or vapor, and may sometimes be incomplete or patchy. Sometimes strange lights or shadows are seen.

Small, spherical "ghost lights" are frequently reported floating about in haunted locations. Unexplained smells are also common; these may vary from the smell of tobacco or perfume to terrible smells of rotting flesh or sulphur. Staircases, bedrooms, and bathrooms are common places for ghost sightings. Lights turning themselves on and off, pictures falling from the walls, and sounds of voices speaking, or screams or moans, are also frequently reported. In poltergeist cases, rapping noises may emanate from the walls, objects may fly across the room, and fires may start spontaneously. These are the terrifying events which have sent many families fleeing from their homes.

There are three major theories that are typically advanced by scientists, spiritualists, and paranormal researchers to account for the experiences reported in haunted houses. Apart from deliberate hoaxes, which researchers agree do occasionally occur, the major theories are as follows:

1. The Psychological Theory. Apparitions and other experiences reported in so-called haunted locations are due to known psychological processes, such as delusions and hallucinations. Although diagnosed mental disorders are sometimes seen in those who report such experiences, mentally healthy individuals are also prone to occasional hallucinations and false beliefs. Mass hysteria can account for the cases in which multiple witnesses report similar experiences. According to this theory, it is not necessary to seek paranormal or supernatural explanations for such experiences, as the psychological mechanisms that are responsible are fairly well understood by scientists, even if not by the majority of laypeople. A variation of this theory suggests that certain environmental factors—such as the presence of unusual electromagnetic fields—may trigger hallucinations

and delusions in certain individuals whose brains are particularly sensitive to such factors. The psychological theory assumes that reports of objects moving by themselves and other physical effects are either imaginary or explained by more mundane causes, such as earth tremors, gusts of wind, and so on.

2. The Spiritistic Theory. This theory is the most popular one, embraced by much of the public as well as by the majority of amateur paranormal investigators. The theory asserts that the phenomena reported in hauntings are caused by disembodied or non-corporeal entities. Although spirits of the dead are most often implicated in hauntings, other variants of this theory include demons and extra-dimensional beings. Most investigators who embrace this theory assume that the physical effects reported in hauntings are genuine, and that ghosts can be photographed or otherwise recorded under certain circumstances.

3. The Parapsychological Theory. This theory incorporates elements of the other two theories. Most academically oriented parapsychologists (myself included) regard this theory as the one that best explains the majority of the facts known about haunting cases. It assumes that although psychological factors can and do account for many of the reported experiences in haunting cases, there are at least some cases in which genuine paranormal factors are involved. For example, an apparition may be regarded as a type of hallucination, as suggested by the psychological theory, but some of these hallucinations include an element of extrasensory perception (ESP) or psychokinesis (PK). This would explain why witnesses to apparitions may sometimes acquire accurate information about the history of a particular

location, which they could not have had access to previously. This theory also suggests that reported physical effects such as percussive sounds or movement of objects in poltergeist cases, are sometimes genuine, but are due to psychokinesis (mind over matter) directed by the mind of one or more living people, not by demons or spirits of the dead.

As a parapsychologist, I come into contact with many reports of haunted houses. One case that illustrates the psychological factors involved in haunting cases concerns a family who lived in an affluent suburb of Atlanta, Georgia. The recurring phenomena that they reported occurred at night, and involved the mother and daughter hearing footsteps across the wooden floor of the dining room, up the stairs, and stopping outside the teenage daughter's bedroom. Upon investigation, no one was there. The family made discreet inquiries with the neighbors about the history of the house. They were told that no one ever stayed there for very long. When I investigated the case it was clear that the present occupants believed that the ghost of a past resident, whom they were certain had died in the house, was responsible for the phenomena. They assured me that these occurrences had also apparently been experienced by previous occupants of the house, with the result that no one ever stayed there for long. An hour in the local records office showed that, despite what the neighbors had said, a normal number of families had stayed in the house over a reasonable period of time and, even though some of the past occupants may have died, there was no evidence to suggest that they had died in the house. This illustrates the point that when faced with apparently unexplained phenomena, many people jump to the conclusion that the only explanation could be the spirit of a past resident who died in the house. In this case, the family's belief was reinforced by neighbors who appeared to have invented a spurious history of the house.

I was eventually able to trace the sounds of the footsteps in this case to a perfectly natural cause. The central heating system—which tended to switch on automatically after dark due to the cooler temperature—was causing the hardwood floors to expand in a sequential manner, beginning on the lower floor of the house (which cooled more quickly) and gradually making its way up the wooden stairs to the hallway above. The sounds made by the expanding floorboards did indeed sound uncannily like footsteps. Even when faced with such contradictions, however, the family was convinced that a death must have taken place in the house. The house had become a sort of psychic scapegoat. Sometimes, rumors that a house is haunted can lead a family to a kind of hyper-vigilance, in which normal sounds are perceived as signs of a tormented spirit. Before long, the entire family is convinced that a house that everyone was happy to live in prior to the rumors is haunted.

I investigated a similar case recently. Again the occupants were concerned that someone had died in the house, and that his or her spirit was responsible for the phenomena. The investigation undertaken along with other researchers from the American Institute of Parapsychology strongly indicated that an unusual but completely natural electromagnetic phenomenon was responsible for the events. Nevertheless, the occupants still desperately believed that a supernatural explanation was more probable. This case also illustrates a very important and often overlooked aspect of hauntings. Throughout the years, I have found many similar cases in which a more positive outlook on life, based on the possibility of life after death, is developed by some witnesses to the paranormal. The family in question have since moved to a small rural community, and both parents are now actively involved in various aspects of psychic healing. After enduring what they have described as a living nightmare, the family has emerged stronger for it.

One motif that emerges in many cases is the apparent link between hauntings and poltergeist disturbances, and adolescents going through puberty, usually with additional family problems thrown into the mix. The most common psychological themes in such cases are repressed aggression and tensions within the family. Such cases provide substantial evidence for the view that poltergeist phenomena express emotions and conflicts that are collectively denied or repressed by the other family members. In my experience, apparent paranormal occurrences associated with hauntings and poltergeist cases are nearly always reported during crisis periods within a dysfunctional family environment. Although parapsychologists do not yet have enough data to draw any concrete conclusions at present, we can speculate that in case of haunting and poltergeists, we are dealing with frustrated and repressed creative tendencies, which, due to external and internal psychological factors, can be projected onto the immediate environment. It is difficult for those who have not lived in a haunted house to appreciate the emotions and stress involved, so we should not be surprised that witnesses often find it easier to believe that spirits are involved, rather than something much closer to home.

Recent consciousness research has led to investigations of geomagnetic fields and other so-called earth energies at ancient sites. Research conducted by Paul Devereux[1] in the UK suggests strong correlations between the locations of stone circles and other sacred sites and geological faulting, as well as with unusual magnetic field properties that are typically associated with such features. This research involved volunteers sleeping and dreaming at selected ancient sites to see if any dream motifs would emerge that could shed new light on the relationship between these sites and the dream experiences. Canadian neuroscientist Michael Persinger has also done a great deal of work linking altered states of consciousness, anomalous experiences, and the influence of man-made electromagnetic fields on the human mind. My own research, along with that of several other parapsychologists, suggests that such anomalous magnetic fields are often associated with hauntings, as well.

The research involving dream content at sacred sites can be equally applied to the study of haunted houses. One of the under-developed areas of parapsychological research which I am now pursuing is the interaction of human consciousness with haunted locations. Writing in the 1920s, Jung made a pertinent observation: "One of the most important sources of the primitive belief in spirits is dreams."[2] I began this approach because I came across numerous cases of hauntings in which one or more of the witnesses reported having vivid dreams that only occurred in the house, never while they were away. These dreams often seemed related to historical aspects of the house or location. If we look beyond the obvious personal and emotional aspects of the dreams, we can begin to glimpse some paranormal details with strong shamanistic elements. Ancestor dreams, out-of-body experiences, encounters with spirits or other apparitional figures (often with a message for the living), are all apparent in shamanic practices. However, the study of witnesses' dreams tends to be overlooked by most paranormal investigators, which is unfortunate, because I suspect that dreams are the key to unlock many of the mysteries of haunted houses. Jung had similar thoughts when he said that "the primitive speaks of spirits, the European speaks of dreams."[3] I am convinced that if a typical modern person were obliged to go through the same exercises and ceremonies that the medicine man performs in order to make the spirits visible, he or she would have the same experiences. He or she would interpret them differently, of course, and probably devalue them as mere dreams or hallucinations. Perhaps in the case of haunted houses, we can glimpse the emergence of a much neglected strand of shamanic experience. After all, if we placed these experiences within any other context than a modern one, dreams and spirits would be the domain of the shaman.

My own investigations of reputedly haunted locations focus on the individuals involved in the haunting. The goal is not to prove or disprove the existence of ghosts, but to assist those who live in such environments and are experiencing disturbing phenomena. I employ an experience-centered approach, which I refer to as "humanistic parapsychology." Similar to most psychical investigators, I am rarely privileged to observe a disturbance in progress. I base my conclusions on the testimony given by the residents of the troubled house and assess it critically based on the patterns I've seen in other cases or those reported by other investigators. One pattern that has become clear after hundreds of investigations is that the human mind can and often does create astounding and vivid projections which are responsible for many of the experiences reported in haunted locations. Jung called these projections "exteriorized autonomous complexes," and the visual and auditory effects they produce "catalytic exteriorizations." He rejected the idea that any of it originated in the spirit world. In such cases, there is always one or more focal persons around whom the psychic disturbances seem to revolve. No phenomenon can be created or projected without a living subconscious mind to act as a catalyst. I am convinced that the focal person in a haunting is that catalyst in the majority of cases. If this is true, it follows that no one knows more about the identity of the ghost or the underlying purpose of the haunting than the person whose mind is being used in this manner. However, that information lies beneath the threshold of consciousness, so the focal person is unaware of his or her role in producing the haunting effects.

Readers familiar with the so-called Philip Experiment know that it is possible to will a ghost into existence. In the 1970s, members of the Toronto Society for Psychical Research, under the direction of Professor A.R.G. Owen, created a being identified as Philip. The imaginary ghost was supplied with a fictional set of characteristics and family history. Although there was never any doubt that Philip was an imaginary construct, he mystified the group by communicating with them by a series of clearly audible raps on the séance table. His communications included details of his fictional biography as devised by the group. Subsequently, several other researchers have created interactive artificial ghosts using the methods perfected by the Toronto group. One practical application of this approach is the possibility of eliminating paranormal disturbances at haunted locations. Using similar methods, I have developed a technique for "dehaunting" houses which I have used successfully in many cases throughout the years.

When misidentified natural events, a mental aberration, or fraud cannot account for a haunting, and when the residents of the troubled house request that I get rid of the disturbances (and when, in my judgment, it appears feasible to do so), my objective is to reach the focal person's subliminal level of consciousness. I am seeking clues to the identity of the ghost, the reasons for its presence, and the opportunity to plant a strong suggestion—a psychological block—against the subconscious use of ghostly projections. In my experience, such blocks create an effective and lasting mental shield against psychic phenomena. To achieve these goals I use a system designed to stimulate subconscious responses. I create the atmosphere of a séance combined with techniques borrowed from Gestalt psychology and hypnotherapy. I refer to this technique as a *psi session*. (The Greek letter *psi* is the symbol for "psychic" or "parapsychological.") The psi session is a very useful tool for the parapsychologist, but because the impressionable and unsophisticated are sometimes strongly affected by it, it must be conducted with great care. To the uninformed, the phenomena experienced in a séance can seem almost magical.

The psi session has all of the trappings of the séances performed a century ago except that I do not normally employ the services of a medium. Instead, I encourage the members of the family—particularly the focus person—to act as their own mediums. By directly involving the person who is the center of the disturbance, the need for a professionally trained sensitive is eliminated. One reason I decided to tap the subconscious of the focus person rather than use a medium is that professional psychics tend to pick up intuitive material that has little or nothing to do with the investigation. Misidentified perceptions only add more confusion to a situation already saturated with it. Furthermore, mediumistic communications seem to be limited by the extent of the medium's knowledge and vocabulary. Often his or her personality and presuppositions negatively affect the situation. However, because the focus person is directly involved with the haunting, he or she is apt to produce information that is related to it. In those situations in which I've employed the psi session, I have observed a high rate of success in tapping the more direct and accurate source of information, the focus.

The goal of the psi session is to reach the source of the disturbances. One method is to allow the mind of the participants to create subconscious movements called "automatisms." Automatisms affect the movement of various psychic tools such as the pendulum, Ouija board, automatic writing planchette, and the "table tilting" effects often observed during séances. Psychologists call this process *ideomotor signaling*, and hypnotists often use it to encourage non-vocal, involuntary responses from hypnotized subjects. Professional psychic readers become adept at picking up involuntary hints and non-verbal cues as they move from one supposition to another. Their impressive accuracy may lead one to believe they are truly legit, when in fact the bulk of the factual material comes from the subject's own non-verbal actions. Although many psychics are genuinely gifted, paranormal investigators should be aware of the existence of automatic functioning and develop the skill of interpreting non-verbal, involuntary feedback. Although some of the techniques of hypnotherapy are employed in the psi session, it is not an exercise in hypnotism. It is not necessary to induce a trance in someone to get him or her to operate the devices of the séance. It only requires a willingness to follow directions; automatisms will typically do the rest. Tools such as a pendulum or writing planchette access the recesses of the mind, amplifying tiny motor signals from the subconscious and converting them into meaningful messages.

During a psi session, four to six participants are seated around a table illuminated by candlelight. Again, although the session typically involves multiple sitters, the procedure is actually directed at the focus person or persons. During this procedure I repeat questions and wait for replies through the automatic writing of the planchette, or the simple yes-or-no responses of the pendulum. Similar to the pointer of a Ouija board, the writing planchette is a small triangular platform with tripod legs, except that the leg at the apex is replaced by a pencil or pen. The two rear legs are fitted with small wheels or ball bearings to facilitate ease of movement. The device rests on a large pad of paper, while the fingertips of the participants rest lightly on the surface of the planchette. In this manner it writes out words or draws pictures while being guided by the subconscious minds of the participants. My goal is to uncover who or what is responsible for the haunting and what I can do to end it. Initially, a number of meaningless words or jumbles of letters may be produced; later messages may consist of letters arranged in reverse order (mirror-writing). However, with persistent questioning, the messages usually become clearer, and the synthesized spirit, which is the source of the haunting, will reveal itself.

Between the 1850s and the turn of the 20th century, table tilting was a popular pastime in many Victorian homes. When used in the psi session, it can produce exciting and sometimes disconcerting effects. Using a lightweight card table resting on a smooth surface, I ask the sitters to place their hands lightly on the table surface, with their palms down and fingers spread apart in such a way that their little fingers are touching. With verbal suggestions from me, the table may rear up off the floor, seemingly levitating or pirouetting on one or two legs. This is an impressive demonstration, but its value for solving the mystery of the haunting is minimal. Tables move for the same reason that pendulums and planchettes do: the process of motor automatism.

Although the mechanics of automatisms are well understood, there is no actual proof of the source of the messages. There is always the possibility that messages originating in the spirit world are bypassing consciousness and directly affecting the muscles of the arm and hand. However, in the majority of haunting cases, the evidence clearly points to a living, human (albeit subconscious) origin for the haunting phenomena. The goal of the psi session is to reach the subliminal level of consciousness and block the minds of the participants from being used or abused by the offending ghost. This is also called *reframing*, a term hypnotherapists use to describe a change in a particular pattern of behavior by working directly with the subconscious without using the conscious mind as an intermediary.

Using suggestion, I attempt to change the patterns that have caused the haunting phenomena to be exteriorized. Where the victims believe their haunting is caused by a spirit invader, I will address the spirit during the psi session and attempt to persuade it to "move on to the other side." In cases where the source of the haunting is insufficiently moved to cease and desist without the use of stronger language, I fall back on commands to depart borrowed from the formal rite of exorcism. (Most of my work is carried out without the need for séances or biblical exhortations, however.) The psi session does not always succeed in permanently eliminating the haunting, however. Sometimes additional sessions are required. In addition, I always recommend that the haunted family seek counseling to address the issues which, in my opinion, led to the haunting in the first place. In the majority of cases, however, anticipation and the right atmosphere tend to produce not only useful information through automatisms, but an environment ripe for the command that the haunting will end. From a therapeutic standpoint, it hardly matters if the haunting is caused by a spirit returned from the dead or a thought-form projected by one or more of the haunted family. The psi session works in either case.

For too long now, most paranormal investigators (or, as the tabloids still insist on calling us, "ghost busters") have concentrated on the technological approach to haunting investigations, focusing on the use of various pieces and types of recording equipment with, frankly, very limited results. What has often been overlooked in the past has been the psychological aspect of hauntings, and that is because the haunted house still remains the domain of the amateur investigator, while most professional parapsychologists are more concerned with repeatable PK and ESP experiments in their laboratories and academic settings. This is unfortunate because with a cooperative effort, we have a greater chance of reaching a better understanding of hauntings. The amateur ghost hunters also do not seem to be coming up with the goods, tending instead to stick with the same old concept of spirits.

The few parapsychologists who specialize in spontaneous cases are aware that we need to take a new look at ghosts and hauntings. New ideas must be proposed and tested. Many academic investigators persist in adopting a skeptical or non-committal stance to avoid criticism. As a parapsychologist with many years of investigating haunting and poltergeist cases behind me, I have come to question how we interpret ghosts and, more specifically, the haunted house. I do not profess to have the ultimate solution to this mystery, but I do hope to stimulate rational discussion of a subject that has remained on the fringes long enough.

Notes

1. Paul Devereux, *Earth Memory: Sacred Sites—Doorways into Earth's Mysteries* (St. Paul, Minn.: Llewellyn Publications, 1992).

2. Jung, C.G., *Psychology and the Occult.* (Princeton, N.J.: Princeton University Press, 1981), 108–125.

3. Ibid.

Not Quite Dead: When a Ghost Is Not Really a Ghost

By Larry Flaxman and Marie D. Jones

"Dude, run!"

—Brian Harnois, *Ghost Hunters* (Season 1, Episode 5)

Every weekend, thousands of dedicated people the world over get together to take part in a growing social and cultural collective experience known as ghost hunting. People from all walks of life—young and old, conservative and liberal, skeptic and believer—load up their cameras, recorders, cables, batteries, and all manner of technical gadgets and gizmos designed to find physical "evidence" or proof of life after death. They head out to private residences (usually older homes that have developed a spooky reputation), cemeteries, and even historical sites steeped in tales of the long-dead spirits that continue to haunt the location, eager to find the smoking gun that will prove that we don't really die and that in some form, in some way, we continue on long after we pass through death's door and go toward the light. Some are searching for answers, while others are merely searching for the next thrill or adventure.

Regardless, with more than 150 years of serious paranormal research behind us, beginning with the age of Spiritualism and continuing up until the modern-day success of paranormal "reality" TV shows that depict police officers, plumbers, and college students alike tracking down spirits, we still are no closer to truly understanding what ghosts are, where they come from, how they manifest on the physical plane, and why they choose to do so in the first place. Maybe, just maybe, we are looking for ghosts in all the wrong places. As Albery Szent-Györgyi once said, "Discovery consists of seeing what everybody has seen and thinking what nobody has thought." Perhaps we are looking for ghosts that aren't really ghosts at all.

Throughout the years, enthusiasts, researchers, and investigators of the paranormal have proposed numerous ideas and theories about what ghosts are. Before we can begin to examine several of the more popular concepts currently being discussed, it may be helpful to understand exactly what this enigmatic label, *ghost*, entails. According to Merriam-Webster, the term means "a disembodied soul; especially: the soul of a dead person believed to be an inhabitant of the unseen world or to appear to the living in bodily likeness." As you can see, the term is inextricably linked with death. Ghost equals dead person? Perhaps, but what if ghosts were *not* always the spooky, chain-rattling spirits of departed souls? There are actually several theories that have been posited to explain the phenomenon. Let's examine several of the more popular ones.

Theory 1: Ghosts are the earthbound spirits of the deceased. To many, this theory creates more questions than it answers, but it is still the gold standard that guides most ghost hunters and paranormal researchers as they apply their investigative methodologies. This is certainly one of the most popular theories, and one for which there has been a great deal of anecdotal and experiential evidence recorded throughout the ages. Ask around and invariably someone you know will tell you of his or her deeply personal experience where they believe they have seen, heard, felt, or even smelled a departed loved one. This concept could clearly be used to explain visual anomalies in which a relative or friend is recognized after death. Some researchers believe that these types of hauntings may be prescient or precognitive in nature, as many of these experiences impart or transfer vital information to the living. We know from the theories of quantum mechanics—specifically, Einstein's "spooky action at a distance" and quantum entanglement—that two objects, once entangled, can still influence each other even when they are separated, with no known intermediary. Is it a stretch to believe that human beings can likewise become "entangled," perhaps via some unknown result of emotional bonding, while continuing to influence each other over vast physical (or even etheric) distances? Are we connected in a grid-like infrastructure, and could this connection transcend life itself?

In terms of how energy behaves, we do know from the first law of thermodynamics that energy does not cease to exist; rather, it changes form within a system or transfers to another system. If ghosts truly are the essence of the dead, what is they were simply the energy appearing to us from within the construct of a different system, where matter and form are not purely physical? Then again, the quantum world tells us we are not solid, either, but we are still alive. There is so much about energy and matter that we have yet to understand before we can truly determine what happens to our soul, and even our consciousness, when we die.

This law might also help explain ghostly apparitions of inanimate objects, such as cars, trains, and mysterious ships that have appeared to people for centuries. "Ghosts" of objects are exempt from the same considerations as ghosts of once-living things with a life force, but they still have energy that has somehow been transformed within this system. Inanimate objects that continue to appear to people in haunted locations speak more of the possibility of stored or imprinted energy, or even a holographic projection that is "looped" into the environment from another, higher dimension.

But these cars and trains and ships are not dead, per se—just no longer moving along the roads, tracks, and oceans of the present. Perhaps time distortion, time slips, and even time travel plays a role in these sorts of apparitions. Are the people who are fortunate enough to witness them getting a sneak peek into another dimension of time, where these vehicles once traveled the roads and waterways they now haunt? Apparitions of this sort might be referred to as *warps*, in the terminology of Joshua Warren, who documented them in his book *How to Hunt Ghosts*. Again, this is the simplest and most popular theory. Ghosts are the spirits of people who once walked the earth and are now dead; they can also be apparitions of objects that were once in existence but are now defunct.

Theory 2: Ghosts and other apparitions are created by naturally occurring environmental conditions such as electricity and electromagnetic radiation. For years, ghost hunters have used technology as a means to measure and analyze environmental factors that might be conducive to a paranormal event. The unfortunate fact here is that the vast majority of paranormal researchers are hobbyists with no formal background or training in basic science, let alone the complex and often fluid nature of environmental analysis. As the old saying goes, owning a box of crayons does not instantly make one an artist. At any rate, the most popular tool used by hobbyist ghost hunters is the EMF, or electromagnetic field meter. This device, originally designed for measuring AC or DC electromagnetic field strength, is often (and incorrectly) used to "prove" that a ghost is present. While most consumer grade meters on the market measure the electromagnetic radiation flux density of DC fields, or the difference in an AC field over time, they essentially function as a type of simple radio antenna, albeit with distinct detection abilities. Interestingly, most meters are calibrated to measure 50hz or 60hz, which is the frequency of U.S. and European AC *mains electricity* (the general-purpose power

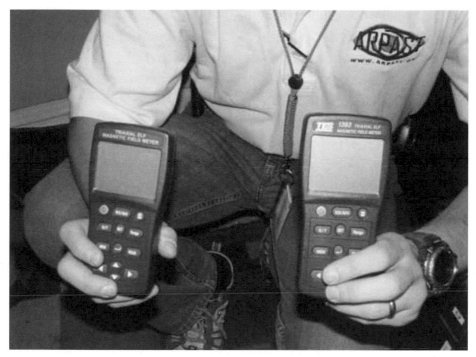

Two of the EMF meters used by paranormal investigators.

supply). It is unclear who originally came up the idea that electromagnetic fluctuation equals ghost, but it is patently obvious that they had little scientific grounding.

It certainly looks cool on television when a ghost hunter excitedly "detects" a ghost based solely on an elevated electromagnetic reading; however, to date there have been no legitimate scientific studies performed that conclusively link fluctuations in EM fields to ghosts or any other paranormal phenomenon. That said, electromagnetic fields may play a role in the *perception* of ghosts, although perhaps not in the way you would think. We know from research studies performed by such luminaries as Dr. Michael Persinger (creator of the so-called God helmet) that low-level electromagnetic energy can and does affect the physiology of the human body in very unusual ways. The human nervous system works via electrical impulses, and anything that could potentially alter or modify normal signal transmission could potentially bring about anomalous perceptions and experiences. Other environmental elements such as temperature, humidity, barometric pressure, air ion count, and particulate count may also play a role in such perceptions and experiences. Some of the more fringe researchers believe that environmental factors may actually serve to open some type of gateway or portal, thereby allowing paranormal phenomena to make their way into our reality.

Investigations conducted by legitimate, science-based field research organizations, such as Larry's team, ARPAST (Arkansas Paranormal and Anomalous Studies Team—*www.arpast.org*), show promise in the area of correlating experiential paranormal events with environmental triggers. One recent investigation was conducted at a reportedly haunted location—a church, no less! This historic building, constructed around the turn of the previous century, has been the site of all manner of paranormal reports throughout the years. From the traditional apparition sightings and unusual noises and sounds to people feeling dizzy and nauseous, this site certainly had the potential to make for an interesting investigation.

After we had conducted our initial walk-through to familiarize ourselves with the floor plan and general layout, we conducted an initial evaluation to determine the church's baseline environmental characteristics such as temperature and humidity levels, the amount of airborne particulate matter present, electromagnetic field strength, air/ion count, and mold spore presence. During this baseline phase, we log and capture data regarding 17 different environmental points. Nothing significant was noted. Next, we split up into four groups to deploy additional monitoring equipment that allowed us a more granular view of the environmental conditions present throughout the location. It was during this equipment deployment that we discovered something very unusual. In the room that had the most reported paranormal activity, we set up a prototype ELF (extremely low frequency) antenna array connected to a real-time FFT (Fast Fourier Transform) spectrum analyzer. This custom device provides us with a glimpse into segments of the electromagnetic spectrum that are invisible when using more traditional ghost-hunting equipment. In fact, this system allows us to measure and quantify energy types and sources that normally evade of the capabilities of most consumer-level devices. Upon initiating the data capture, we were presented almost immediately with an interesting and unique localized electromagnetic profile. Throughout this particular room we noted a very consistent 19hz peak. A 19hz standing wave? Did this particular infrasonic frequency have any significance?

In our second book, *The Resonance Key: Exploring the Links Between Vibration, Consciousness and the Zero Point Grid*, we talked about research conducted by Vic Tandy, a professor at Coventry University in England, who suggested that 19hz might be responsible for some experiential paranormal events. Professor Tandy was working late one evening at a laboratory at Warwick. Although he had heard all of the stories and rumors about the lab being haunted, as a man of science he generally dismissed them as folly. This evening proved to be different, however. Tandy certainly could not ignore the gray shapeless mass that he detected out of the corner of his eye. It seemed to move throughout the room, but when he followed it to investigate, there was nothing there. The next day, again while in the lab, Tandy was seated at a workbench, working on his fencing foil which was clamped into a vise. With nothing touching the foil, the blade began to vibrate violently. Further analysis led Tandy to ascertain that the fan in the lab was emitting a frequency of 18.98hz, which was very close to the resonant frequency of the viscous fluid in the human eye— 19hz! The night before, Tandy wasn't "seeing" a ghost—he was experiencing an optical illusion caused by his eyeballs resonating. Because of this, 19 Hz would soon come to be known as the "ghost frequency."

Extensive research has shown that infrasonic energy causes distinct physiological reactions in the human body. Some of the more common effects on the human central nervous system include nausea, vertigo, disorientation, auditory shifts, tactile sensitivity change, vestibular (inner ear) effects such as vertigo, and hypothermia. Many of these effects are commonly reported as "proof" of the paranormal. For instance, hypothermia could easily be correlated with the so-called cold spots often reported during hauntings. Nausea, disorientation, auditory shifts (hearing things)—again, these are all textbook effects. Interestingly, in the period of time that we were in this room, several investigators had to leave the area because they felt physically ill. One was nauseous, and one had what he described as a migraine headache.

Theory 3: Ghosts are simply the "playback" of energy or stored human emotion that was once present in the location and then somehow captured or "recorded" into the environment. This theory is most often referenced when discussing a *residual haunting*, which is often thought of as the most common type of haunting—most typically a visual or auditory signature that has somehow been imprinted (or recorded) into the environment and then "played back" in a continuous loop. This phenomenon is usually attributed to a visual manifestation appearing to replicate the same actions continually, similar to someone pressing Rewind and Play repeatedly. From a scientific perspective, we know from the first law of thermodynamics that matter and energy can neither be created nor destroyed; it can only change form, as in solid to liquid, but the total amount of matter and energy in the universe remains constant and fixed. The second law of thermodynamics says that although the quantity of matter and energy remains the same, the *quality* deteriorates over time. Incidentally, there are countless reports that detail sightings of faded or semi-translucent apparitions, many of which appear to blink in and out of view, as if the energy behind the apparition were not consistent in strength. Furthermore, this theory begs the question of whether human emotion may be a form of energy itself, and whether this energy would be powerful enough to somehow be imprinted onto the environment. Although the mechanics of this theory have neither been explained nor scientifically proven, it would seem to support many of the accounts of residual hauntings. Perhaps the energy that is imprinted upon certain locations plays itself out at a specific frequency or vibratory level, much like a movie projecting the same scene over and over until someone turns off the projector.

This theory might also be applied to EVP, or electronic voice phenomena, in which words and phrases are captured onto digital voice recorders after ghost hunters and investigators pose questions such as "What is your name?" and "Why are you trapped here?" The idea is that, somehow, the entities, wherever they may be, still have the ability to speak, or that the verbiage, like the image, has somehow been trapped and imprinted upon the particular location in a never-ending loop. In our opinion, we also need to think about EVP from the standpoint of the investigators: Are we really picking up the actual voices of the dead, or merely the thoughts and feelings of the investigators?

Theory 4: Ghosts, spirits, and other phenomena are very much alive and active, but present in alternate dimensions or realities. Let's suppose for a moment that everything that we think we know about reality is wrong. What if there were multiple levels of reality and corresponding forms of life on each of these different levels? Believe it or not, this may be less speculative than you realize. Way back in 1895, the American philosopher

ALLEN PARK PUBLIC LIBRARY #4

and psychologist William James coined the term *multiverse* to refer to a hypothetical set of possible universes and realities. According to the theory, these universes comprise the entirety of time, space, energy, and matter, each with its own set of physical laws and constants. Imagine the possibilities! Perhaps there exists a world without gravity—or one in which we breathe methane rather than oxygen. The multiverse theory was later expanded by cosmologist Max Tegmark, who postulated a taxonomy of universes beyond the observable universe, and helped to pave the way for other theoretical constructs such as M-Theory and Everett's "many worlds" interpretation.

While encompassing various functional differences, fundamentally, the various theories all point to the possibility of multiple realities and/or dimensions. In fact, scientists have postulated that space may actually be comprised of 11 dimensions. Although we can only perceive three spatial dimensions, is it possible that everything we brand as "paranormal" may in fact be "normal" in one or more of those other eight dimensions? If a ghostly apparition is indeed coming to us from another dimension or parallel universe, it might not be a dead person we are seeing at all, but a real, live person whom we are merely glimpsing across the great divide of reality. We might also be seeing time travelers, people from the past or the future, appearing to us as erratic, flickering, fuzzy, and ghostly images of what on the other side is a perfectly solid person. This theory might also apply to ghost trains, planes, and automobiles, all of which may be actively operating in other levels of reality, as well.

It has also been theorized that this playback of events might also support the holographic universe theory insofar as what we generally consider to be our three-dimensional reality might in actuality be a projection from a higher dimensional source. It is certainly possible that ghosts are images or projections flickering on the "screen" of our reality—elusive and erratic, perhaps, because they are coming from somewhere else entirely. Think of taking your significant other to the movies and watching the story unfold before your eyes on the big screen. The tableau is actually a projection of still pictures coming from above the balcony area, where the projectionist sits and operates the projection machinery.

Theory 5: Ghosts are merely figments of our own creative imaginations. This theory is also known as the "it's all in our heads" theory. Taking into account the thousands of reported incidents as well as the similarity among them, this suggestion seems silly on the surface, particularly because ghosts and other anomalous phenomena have been documented and described since the dawn of time. Have every single one of these reports simply been fanciful imaginings or hallucinations? This seems unlikely. Or, is it possible that our brains are somehow responsible for designing these scenarios, based upon an external stimulus or influence?

Recall the work of Dr. Persinger, whose God helmet was able to induce in subjects what he termed the "sensed presence" of something in the room with them, rather than an actual physical manifestation. In addition, Persinger's helmet induced numerous test subjects to experience incredibly vivid religious and paranormal imagery simply via the application of low-level electromagnetic signals to the temporal lobe of the brain. What if our brain were simply manufacturing the entire story and plot, perhaps, much like Persinger's helmet, facilitated and enhanced by an as yet unseen external source? The idea of the brain being responsible for these perceptions (and for our overall subjective reality) actually ties in quite nicely with the next theory, namely, that specific chemicals within the brain may be responsible for the creation of these events. We might also ask if this kind of perceptual phenomenon might be the product of the collective unconscious so often referred to by Carl Jung and others, who believe(d) that there is a unified "field" of thoughts and beliefs common to all people. Could ghosts represent an archetype of our collective fear and anxiety regarding death and the nothingness that follows? Have we all bought into this belief and thus created ghosts as proof that we don't simply fade to black when we die? Ashes to ashes, dust to dust?

Symbolic images such as angels and demons also play into the collective unconscious and resonate with us on an intuitive level, perhaps even more so than on an intellectual one. Thus, we might think of ghosts as one of these symbols collectively chosen to represent "life after death" for all of humanity. And of course such a symbol would by necessity appear intangible, ethereal, vague, and elusive, because it represents the unknown (death), which itself is shadowy and unknowable.

This idea also ties into quantum physics and the *observer effect*, which states that we as observers are actually collapsing the wave function of reality into fixed, particulate states. By way of explanation, everything at the quantum level exists as both wave and particle in a state of superposition, until we observe or measure, and thus "collapse," the waveform, pinpointing the particles into fixed positions. This *must* happen, because we cannot know with certainty the momentum or position of a particle without first fixing it into place so we can measure it, which in turn prevents us from knowing its momentum. Ergo, what if we, the investigators and witnesses, were actually observing ghosts into existence because we expect or desire to do so? There is some evidence, though not what we would call proof, that ghost hunting participants are often "fed" information about a particular location, and that a large percentage of those participants then report the very experiences they were told to expect. Is this the power of suggestion at work? Or is it the work of the observer effect, in which several people at once collectively collapse the wave function and observe what they expect or were told to expect (i.e. a ghost)?

What roles do preconception and expectation play in this equation? If you are told that the location you are in is haunted, or if you are grieving the passing of a loved one, would you be more likely to have a paranormal experience? Perhaps the trauma and emotion of dealing with death might be the trigger that allows someone who wants to see a ghost so badly to actually see one. And the same can be said for a room full of eager participants on a highly paid ghost hunt with two guys from a big TV show, who are told they are entering a highly active location and will be locked down inside it all night. The chances are very good they will experience *something*. But the question is, is what they are experiencing really happening, or did they collectively create it? Based on this theory, everyone who loses a loved one or is afraid of creepy old houses should be seeing ghosts, but of course this is not always the case. Which leads us to the next theory.

Theory 6: Ghosts and other paranormal phenomena are simply hallucinations generated by brain chemicals. Dopamine, serotonin, acetylcholine—these are but a few of the chemical substances present in the incredibly complex human brain. Some researchers believe that the perception of ghosts can be explained simply as a chemically induced hallucination or delusion, a natural drug high from natural chemical substances found in our own brains. We know from research that over- or under-production of certain brain chemicals, such as serotonin and dopamine, are directly responsible for feelings of depression and euphoria. So wouldn't it follow that these same chemicals could be responsible for these kinds of experiences? Interestingly, Peter Brugger, a noted neurologist from the University Hospital in Zurich, Switzerland, has conducted studies showing that a direct correlation exists between increased levels of dopamine and paranormal beliefs. In the experiment, Brugger recruited 20 "believers" and 20 "non-believers," and asked them to distinguish real faces from scrambled faces that were briefly shown on a screen. Next, they performed a similar task by identifying real words from fake ones. Perhaps not surprisingly, the believers were much more likely than the non-believers to see a word or face when there was none. How did the non-believers fare? They were much more likely to miss the *real* faces and words displayed. Next, Brugger administered L-dopa, a drug typically used to treat the symptoms of Parkinson's disease by increasing the levels of dopamine in the brain. Although both groups made more mistakes while under the influence of the drug, the non-believers became more likely to interpret the fake words or scrambled faces as the real thing. This fascinating experiment strongly suggests that enhanced levels of dopamine are associated with paranormal beliefs and experiences. It seems that increased levels of dopamine may help people to see patterns or correlations that don't exist.

In our book *The Déjà vu Enigma*, we discussed the work of Rick Strassman, MD, a psychiatrist from the University of New Mexico School of Medicine. Strassman conducted an 11-year study using DMT (dimethyltrypamine), one of the principal ingredients found in *ayahuasca*, the shaman's brew that causes hallucinogenic trips and visions among both natives and curious tourists eager to see beyond the veil of normal perception. Strassman administered DMT in a laboratory setting to participants, who reported everything from déjà vu experiences, altered states of consciousness, and hallucinations to visions and sensations of presences similar to what one might experience during a paranormal event.

Deep brain stimulation of the hypothalamus region has also been studied and linked to déjà vu phenomenon, suggesting that something might be triggering specific parts of the brain, or certain chemicals found in the brain, into perceiving ghostly apparitions. What that trigger is we don't yet know, as it may be a combination of human physiology (nature) and environmental conditions (nurture) that must be "just right," like the porridge Goldilocks so loved to eat. Even a shadow person, described in the next theory, can be created when the left temporoparietal junction, a specific region of the brain, is stimulated.

The brain is the most complex and most mysterious organ in the human body. We know so little about how it performs its magic. Because we all have differing levels of brain chemicals, and even varying levels of activity in specific parts of our brains, perhaps this explains why some of us see ghosts and some of us don't, even when we are standing side by side in the same location or situation. But as Emerson M. Pugh famously stated, "If the human brain were so simple that we could understand it, we would be so simple that we couldn't."

Theory 7: Ghosts are sentient entities that enjoy vexing and even harming humans. Some ghosts seem to like to mess with us, poking and prodding and pulling hair, or, in many cases, engaging in much more terrifying and violent activity. This is the realm of the poltergeist, the demon, the shadow person, and the djinn. A spate of movies about exorcisms has awakened renewed interest in the more negative and frightening aspects of ghostly activity. Are there demonic entities walking the earth in the guise of spirits and shadow figures, stalking and terrorizing and, in some cases, possessing human beings? Paranormal researchers John Zaffis and Rosemary Ellen Guiley think so. They have written extensively about their work with these darker entities. Guiley, in her latest book with physicist Phil Imbrogno, titled *The Vengeful Djinn: Unveiling the Hidden Agendas of Genies*, links ghostly apparitions with these ancient spirits that have their origin in Middle Eastern lore and mythology, yet in many ways take on aspects of what we might call ghosts or even poltergeists. Djinn are also often associated with demons and shadow people, two other dark entities that people may mistake for the ghosts of the dead.

Zaffis, author of *Shadows of the Dark* (with Brian McIntyre), has worked for years with demons in particular, first studying under his uncle and aunt Ed and Lorraine Warren, both widely respected paranormal researchers and demonologists, and learning from them about spirit possession. Later, he worked with prominent exorcists, studying the work of Roman Catholic priests, monks, rabbis, and Protestant ministers, and their varying beliefs regarding demons and demonic possession. Zaffis has actually assisted with the work of well-known exorcists such as Bishop Robert McKenna, Malachi Martin, and Reverend Jun, and lectures widely on his continuing work.

Shadow people are distinct types of ghostly apparitions that usually appear as dark, featureless, humanlike forms that drift across a room or in and out of doors, and then completely vanish into walls. They have also been called "shadow men" and "shadow folk," and have a more sinister, even malicious aspect to them than the average ghost floating around a room. Witnesses often report a distinct feeling of being observed or psychologically toyed with by these shadowy entities. Author Jason Offutt documents dozens of such creepy cases in his book, *Darkness Walks: The Shadow People Among Us*. Although shadow people may not cause harm or wreak havoc, they do terrify, much more so than the apparition of, say, your dearly departed Aunt Winnie. Other researchers have likened shadow people to everything from reptilian aliens and Men in Black to two-dimensional projections from higher realities meant to control our minds. When it comes to shadow people, shadowy and obscure conspiracy theories abound.

Demons and poltergeists, supposedly two completely different phenomena, take on a much more serious and malevolent aspect. Demonology seems to have regained a lot of favor in the public eye as of late, with a spate of new films and TV shows featuring exorcisms and the possessed. The idea that a dark entity or energy can actually enter a human body and take control of it is one of the most fear-inducing elements of the paranormal. Perhaps equally frightening is poltergeist activity, which takes the form of troublesome spirits that throw things about the room, break windows, and generally make a lot of noise and trouble for anyone unlucky enough to experience one. But generally, poltergeists are not considered ghosts per se, for they appear to be connected to kinetic energy from a human source, or *agent*, and somehow have the ability to manifest dark energy into physical form.

The bottom line is, there may be as many types of ghosts as there are ghost reports. Even when we appear to have some kind of direct communication from a ghost, we cannot know for sure that we are dealing with a spirit of the dead, especially when so many aspects of paranormal activity defy that simple and narrow explanation. With the multitude of theories and thousands of experiential reports, perhaps we are making the question of what they are much more difficult than is necessary. The theory of Occam's razor—*lex parsimoniae* in Latin—states that when you have two competing explanations that make exactly the same prediction as far as the outcome, the one that is the simpler or less complex of the two is usually the correct one. Are ghosts, spirits, and entities simpler than we think? And are they even ghosts at all? The next time you see the ghost of your Uncle George floating around the attic, he may actually be alive and well in another world or another universe, or merely a holographic projection from a higher dimension, where he is enjoying life on a whole new plane of existence. Like all ghosts, Uncle George may not really be dead at all.

Bibliography

Guiley, Rosemary E. and Philip J. Imbrogno. *The Vengeful Djinn. Unveiling the Hidden Agendas of Genies.* Woodbury, Minn.: Llewellyn Publications, 2011.

Jones, Marie D. and Larry Flaxman. *The Déjà vu Enigma: A Journey Through the Anomalies of Mind, Memory and Time.* Franklin Lakes, N.J.: New Page Books, 2010.

———. *The Resonance Key: Exploring the Links Between Vibration, Consciousness and the Zero Point Grid.* Franklin Lakes, N.J.: New Page Books, 2009.

Warren, Joshua P. *How To Hunt Ghosts.* New York: Fireside Books, 2003.

The Problem With Poltergeists

By Dr. Bob Curran

Early in 1710, a traveller in Ireland, journeying between Larne and Carrickfergus in East Antrim, passed by an ancient earthworks close to the roadside. Suddenly and without warning, he was pelted by a shower of stones that seemed to be coming from the direction of the earthen fort. Accompanying the stone shower was the sound of hollow, mocking laughter of numerous voices from somewhere close by. The traveller fled in terror and later related his story, much to the unease of those who listened. Apparently he had not been the first to suffer such an indignity. The few Catholics who lived in this area ascribed such an event to the work of evil fairies, whilst to the Protestant majority it was almost certainly witchcraft. When the phenomenon appeared to move to the nearby Islandmagee Rectory and began to affect the local minister's elderly mother, Mrs. Haltridge, the evil intent of such an unseen force seemed confirmed. The disturbances (which actually marked the beginnings of the Islandmagee witchcraft trials) persisted for well over a year, from 1710 to 1711, after the death of the old woman and after the sinister forces attached themselves to her young relative, Mary Dunbar, before suddenly vanishing altogether. Although the events were locally connected to the witchcraft of certain allegedly malign women of the area, later accounts tried to link it with a pamphlet titled

"Lithobolia, or the Stone Throwing Devil," which had been published in 1698 and dealt with similar events which had occurred at a tavern in New England in 1689. This description placed it firmly within the tradition of stone-throwing and object-moving forces, which today we would certainly class as *poltergeists.*

The word *poltergeist* comes from the German—*poltern,* meaning "to rumble or make noise," and *geist,* meaning "spirit"—which gives us the definition of "a noisy or disruptive ghost." The term is used to describe a disembodied force or energy that attaches itself either to a specific location, such as the old earthworks in the previous account, or to a certain individual, such as Mary Dunbar. These energies are usually violent and destructive in nature, and can take a number of forms. Manifestations may include unexplained knockings or rappings; the moving or breaking of objects; unexplained vibrations in inanimate objects; the disruption of mechanical or electrical equipment; voices or smells not emanating from any identifiable source; and even physical harm of the individual to whom the poltergeist has attached itself. In some cases, the events appear to be random, whilst in others there seems to be some form of supernatural intelligence directing them. Indeed, in some instances the poltergeist is able to answer questions. Most often, as in the Islandmagee case, the phenomenon appears and disappears without explanation or trace.

The poltergeist phenomenon has puzzled folklorists and psychic researchers, both of whom are at a loss to explain its cause. Countless suggestions have been offered, but usually these suggestions have raised more questions than they have answered. And many such "explanations" have ignored some highly important aspects of the activity. For example, how is the phenomenon viewed within the prevailing cultural context in which it occurs? In other words, is it perceived solely in supernatural terms—as an undisputed ghost or phantom—or are other explanations readily offered by those individuals or communities who have experienced it—a natural occurrence or even a trick to gain attention or notoriety, for instance? Moreover, is each case simply a standalone event or isolated occurrence, or is there some form of commonality surrounding the various experiences? And in cases in which a single person is involved, what is the nature of the relationship between the poltergeist and the individual to which it attaches itself? In order to try to examine the poltergeist in the light of these questions, I propose that we should look at three salient cases from different parts of the world.

The Articlave Poltergeist

The first case comes from the village of Articlave in Northern Ireland. It is perhaps one of the best-documented occurrences, appearing as a major story in the prestigious *Irish Times*. Originally built around 1613 by Sir Robert McClelland as part of the overall Plantation of County Derry, Articlave was initially settled by Presbyterian Scots (indeed, at one time no native Irish lived in the village). Even today it boasts a strong Presbyterian ethos. These were stolid, sober, hard-working individuals, not given to flights of fancy about ghosts. Nevertheless, in 1934, a 10-year-old girl in the village, the daughter of a staunch Presbyterian family, began to exhibit signs of poltergeist activity. The farmhouse in which the family lived lay on the very edge of the village and was said to have been built on the site of an old Celtic *rath* (a circular fortified settlement built during the Iron Age or early Middle Ages), one of a number which once dotted the country but had later been destroyed. The activities of the troublesome poltergeist commenced one night after the girl had gone to bed. Needless to say, the events were something of a shock both to the family and to the village itself. Stories of the supernatural goings-on began to spread across Northern Ireland (outdoing even stories of the famous Cooneen Ghost of 1911 in County Fermanagh) and latterly into the Irish Republic. The stories even aroused interest in Dublin. The *Irish Times* sent one of its reports, J.P. Donaghy (his name is given locally as Donnelly), to investigate. Interestingly, no name has ever been given for the family concerned, although it is known locally, and only one member has ever been identified—the young girl in question, whom Donaghy names as "Laura," although that was not her real name. Further, no specific date was given as to when the strange attacks started, except that it may have been around the end of 1933 or the beginning of 1934.

Donaghy travelled north to Articlave, a journey which in 1934 was still something of an undertaking, and found the house readily enough. In his story he describes a solid, two-story, unprepossessing building set a little way back from the main road through the village. He arrived just as a storm was gathering over the surrounding hills. Clouds were swiftly rolling in and a severe wind was rising—all seemingly a dark omen for his visit. The invisible spirit had been making life intolerable for the small tenant farmer, his wife, and his children, two sons and a daughter. Although it had seemingly attached itself to Laura, it was creating mischief in the rest of the household, as well. Everyday articles were moving about the rooms of their own volition, and dishes, cloths, and several glass lamp globes were being tossed about the place with an almost reckless abandon in front of the family. At times there was a persistent knocking throughout the house. Laura herself had been unceremoniously flung out of bed several times, resulting in injury more than once. She claimed she felt as though she were being pinched or bitten, and sometimes felt the sensation of hot needles being pressed into her flesh, both of which had left red marks and welts on her skin. The family, who were upstanding, church-going Presbyterians, were at their wits' end and had summoned a minister to exorcise the phantom, but with no success.

Laura's mother and father greeted Donaghy civilly enough and made him welcome. As night drew on, however, several of their neighbours began to gather in the farmhouse kitchen; ever since the disturbances had begun, several local people had offered to stay with the family each night. Donaghy afterwards admitted that he was somewhat surprised by the nature of the people who had called: they were solid, Presbyterian country people who appeared to know little of ghosts and hauntings. Laura herself was, he said, a shy, plain girl and seemed typical for any other child her age. Donaghy had initially suspected that the whole thing might be a trick to enable to family to gain some form of notoriety or fame, but now he was not so sure. The kitchen, as he describes it, was illuminated by a single oil lamp, which cast long and menacing shadows around the room, adding to the eerie atmosphere. The neighbours stayed for several hours, talking and trying to lighten the mood of the evening before departing for their homes.

Around midnight, three "substantial men" from the local community arrived. These were elders from the local Presbyterian church, and they had come to take over the vigil. The talk around the fire became more serious and was interspersed with prayers and readings from the Bible; according to Donaghy, the aura of religion in the house was almost palpable. The conversation eventually waned and the reporter found himself drifting off to sleep. Outside, the storm, which had been threatening for so long, eventually broke, and rain beat against the windowpanes and lightning flashed on the horizon. The heat of the peat fire made everybody drowsy, however; even the dog under the table dozed off but kept yelping softly to itself as though disturbed by strange dreams.

Around 5 a.m., Donaghy was awoken from a light sleep by a noise from the stairs. Something was clearly about to happen. He followed the family members up the narrow staircase to Laura's bedroom. They found the girl lying in a narrow wooden bed pushed tightly against the stone wall of the house, just below the room's only window. The bedroom was illuminated by two candles, which gave off only meagre light. The mother took up a position by the head of the bed whilst the other family members, Donaghy, and one of the three elders gathered at its foot. Laura lay rigid under her blanket, seemingly terrified; she opened her mouth to say something but her voice failed. Then the sounds started.

There was a low knocking in the room. Donaghy observed that it sounded exactly like knuckles being rapped against woodwork, although it was impossible to tell exactly where it was coming from. Sometimes it seemed to originate from the very foot of the bed, sometimes from the head, and sometimes from somewhere close to the stone wall. At times it was quite loud, while at other times it seemed to fade away. At first it maintained a steady, regular rhythm, although at times it seemed more erratic, quickening to an angry and impatient hammering and then suddenly slowing to a light, methodical tapping. Donaghy looked around the room for some sort of wood that would be able to explain the sound, but saw nothing. At one point he thought that it came from an area about two feet above the floor, but then it seemed to come from higher up the wall. He put his hand to the stonework to see if he could sense any vibration, but felt nothing; as soon as he did so, however, the sound appeared to move to another part of the room. Feeling that it was coming from somewhere either inside or right outside the bedroom, Donaghy looked around for a possible source. Thinking that it might be a tree branch being buffeted by the burgeoning wind against the glass window, he opened the window and looked outside. Although there were a couple of tree branches quite close to the window, he could not be absolutely sure that one of these was the source of the sounds. Nor was there any bird that had settled on the windowsill, tapping against the glass with its beak. He turned back into the room and noted that Laura had remained rigid throughout, eyes wide with terror. Still, there seemed to be no explainable source nearby for the unearthly noise.

The church elder who was present now began to ask the spirit several questions, which it answered with a simple tapping code—one tap for no, two for yes. The questions were based on the personal details of the others in the room (not the family), and concerned facts of which Laura was ignorant. Donaghy himself participated in this, asking the poltergeist to pick out his birthday from a list of dates. This it did correctly. It would not, however, answer any questions about itself—when asked, it only replied with prolonged silence. The candles in the room continually flickered and guttered, sometimes to the edge of extinction, which was taken by the church elder as a sign that the spirit was passing by them.

As the storm passed and daylight began to encroach into the room, the sounds suddenly stopped, and Laura fell into a deep and restful sleep. The reporter, quite shaken by the experience, decided to take his leave. Shortly after that night, the weird rappings and other strange phenomena ceased altogether, and peace returned once again to the remote farmhouse. No formal explanation was ever given for the eerie occurrences, and the mystery remains unsolved to this day. Laura died as an elderly woman in Articlave a number of years ago without saying anything further about the incident, and though her offspring still live in the village, none of them will talk about it. There are only few people in Articlave today, even amongst the older residents, who claim to know about what happened. Donaghy himself never forgot the experience.

So who or what was the Articlave poltergeist? Those who have taken an interest in these events have suggested a number of possible explanations, but none has ever been able to fully explain the phenomenon. Some have attributed it to atmospheric conditions at the time (remember that a storm was brewing when Donaghy arrived at the village), but many have quickly discounted this theory, arguing that the conditions would have had to remain the same over a period of time without he slightest variation or fluctuation in air or temperature. However, we must consider two other possible suggestions, which are based on both the prevailing religion and culture of the area at the time. Local knowledge supposedly derived from one of Laura's brothers (the village of Articlave lies approximately five miles from where I'm writing this) states that the whole occurrence was an elaborate hoax in which the family and community itself took part. The family were facing financial difficulties and were considering selling the house and farm to a neighbour or relative who had expressed interest in buying it. The prospective buyer was a member of the Church of Ireland (Anglican/Episcopalian) which, in the eyes of the close-knit community, was close enough to being Roman Catholic. Rather than have the farmland fall into non-Presbyterian hands, the community and the local church conspired in the hoax in an attempt to scare the purchaser away. A story about a violent ghost connected to the premises was then circulated. Although there were accounts of objects being thrown about and items moving of their own volition, nobody outside the family ever witnessed these events. Indeed, the family was both privy to and an active part of this ruse, and the interest of the *Irish Times* was the final blow which destroyed the proposed deal. Although Donaghy had supposedly concentrated on Laura herself, believing her to be the originator of the deception, it had been the other family members and the church elders who had been implicated in the hoax; the girl had just played along with it. Ultimately the family managed to recoup their losses, and the idea of the "ghost" was dropped. At least that's the explanation that Laura's brother is said to have given, although his statements were never substantiated. All of it is simply hearsay.

Another possible explanation, which has its roots in religion, also has the family at its center. It was widely known that Laura's father and mother were both of an evangelical persuasion and that their home was allegedly used for fervent prayer meetings and Bible lessons. Perhaps, as has been suggested by some local commentators, the intensity and fervour of this "holying" in such a close family and within such a tightly-knit community unconsciously generated some form of emotional or psychic energy, which then manifested itself within the house or perhaps even through the girl herself or another family member. Once again, however, the idea is simply an unproven theory held by some local people today.

Thirdly, it is suggested that Laura somehow unwittingly generated the manifestations herself due to the approach of puberty. Although she was only 10 years old when the occurrences took place, Donaghy describes her as a shy, serious girl well advanced beyond her years. Could it be that as she matured, certain mental and emotional forces somehow burst through that rigid and tightly controlled environment and manifested themselves in the so-called poltergeist activity? Although we may never really know the cause of these events, I will return to this last possible explanation later.

Bouncing Bertha

The case of Bouncing Bertha, although from a different part of the world, is not all that far removed from the Articlave experience. This case contained many similar elements, and it, too, became something of a celebrated occurrence in its locale, the Blue Ridge mountains of Virginia. This case also involved a young pre-pubescent girl living within a close family structure and in a fairly remote area. The events that befell the girl in question in 1938 followed roughly the same pattern as those that had beset Laura in Articlave just four years earlier. However, this case is slightly better documented in that we know the true identities of those involved. The girl's name was Bertha Sybert, and she would later become known in certain areas of the country as "Bouncing Bertha."

The Syberts were ordinary working folk who lived at Wallens Creek in Lee County, deep in the Blue Ridge mountains. They were related to a number of their neighbours, and Bertha's grandmother, "Grandma Jane" Sybert, a sort of family matriarch, lived not all that far away. From her earliest years, Bertha was a lively, cheeky child, very pretty and photogenic. In a photo of the class of 1938 taken at the local school in Sand Springs, she clearly stands out as an unusually pretty 9-year-old, smiling sweetly from the front row amongst some of her more homely classmates, some of whom were her own relatives. Also in the same photograph is Raymond Miner, who was related to the Syberts through marriage, and who would later become the main informant concerning the early stages of Bertha's encounter with what appeared to be supernatural forces. According to him, the eerie phenomena began not long after that school photograph was taken. In fact, it was Raymond, his father, and his uncle who first witnessed the curious phenomena that affected the little girl as she lay in her bed at night.

Bertha Sybert's bedroom seems to have been just as plain and poor as Laura's was in Articlave. Indeed, its walls were "papered" in old newspapers, some of which had been stuffed into cracks to keep out the draught. Her bed was unremarkable, just a wooden frame construction with a small mattress on top. In the winter of 1938, however, the bed seemed to take on a life of its own. At first, Bertha felt a faint tremor running from the top to the bottom, but it slowly increased in strength and frequency, later becoming so violent that Bertha was actually thrown from one side to the other and sometimes even onto the cabin floor. She appeared to have no control over what later became known as the "bouncing bed."

Amongst the first to witness the phenomenon was the Miner family, who were staying with their relatives at the time. Raymond Miner gave a detailed account of what he saw. The events, he said, would start off with a faint whispery sound, like a mouse moving at the headboard of the bed or a rat gnawing at a piece of wood, somewhere in the room. It would move up the cabin wall until it was level with Bertha's bed as she lay between the covers. All the while, the sound would increase both in volume and ferocity. It now sounded like a washboard being hit with a block of wood. On several occasions, he said, he placed his hand to the wall and felt the vibration from it. Then the bed would vibrate and move up and down, bouncing faster and faster until it would almost appear to be dancing, with Bertha bouncing within it. In fact, so rapid and violent was the motion that four strong men standing at each corner of the bed couldn't hold it still. Sometimes it reared and bucked so violently that Bertha was thrown out at their feet. At first it was thought that she was somehow responsible for the strange occurrence, but she lay so rigid between the sheets—doubtless paralyzed with terror—that it seemed impossible that she could contribute in any way to the activity.

There were other strange things going on besides the bouncing bed. Gradually, the makeshift "wallpaper" began to peel from the bedroom walls as the bed vibrated. At one point, according to some reports, a withered human hand with long, ragged fingernails appeared in the air above the girl's head and seemed to swipe at her before vanishing again. Interior doors in the cabin shook and banged violently by themselves. Rank and stomach-churning stenches filled the cabin, and a chair on which Bertha usually sat allegedly appeared to "walk" across a room in front of the family. Although some of the accounts may well have been exaggerated, there is little doubt that the events had badly shaken both the Sybert family and the community. During these occurrences, Bertha never saw her tormentor, although she sometimes complained about a "white fuzzy thing" that was sometimes in the room, and which she could see just out of the corner of her eye. This being, she said, sometimes came to the end of her bed and rocked it. Every time she began to drift off to sleep, the thing, which appeared to have a vaguely human shape, would pull her hair in the most alarming manner.

News about what was happening was now starting to leak out beyond Wallens Creek. Local newspapers began to take an interest, which in turn drew the attention some of the national press. Intrigued by the story, the press gave the girl the nickname "Bouncing Bertha." Like Donaghy in Ireland, a number of reporters made their way to the Blue Ridge mountains to see if they could track down the family and get some sort of explanation for the peculiar phenomena. The situation was somewhat exacerbated by the grandmother-matriarch, Jane Sybert, who allowed herself to be interviewed on several occasions and invited reporters into the little cabin that she'd occupied since 1888. She spoke of "conjure folk" (possibly relatives) living further up in the mountains with whom the Syberts had had a disagreement. Had these people, she asked, "called down" something to cause trouble for the family? She even recounted some old Native American legends which made reference to strange forces that had made their home in the area. These tales of mountain magic only added to the speculation.

In an attempt to put an end to the eerie phenomena, Bertha moved out of the cabin at Wallens Creek and went to live with the Miners. It was thought that if she moved, the bouncing would stop. However, the move was of no use, for the phantom or force appeared to follow her to the new location. Even when Raymond Miner played hymns on his guitar by her bedside, it had no effect. If anything, Bertha's bed began to vibrate even faster and harder. When Raymond changed his music to ragtime, Bertha was literally flung up into the air due to the force.

By that time Bertha had become something of a celebrity. Her name was known far beyond the state line of Virginia. When she went to see her first movie in the local theatre in Jonesville, crowds turned out to see her. She was obviously of more interest than the movie itself, and so, with an eye for business, the theatre had her take the stage and recite an eight-line poem. The entertainment business was not far behind. A promoter named Virgil Wacks took her to Pineville to appear in a Vaudeville show, in which she tried, unsuccessfully, to re-create the "bouncing" experience. The spirit, it seemed, didn't want to cooperate for the benefit of a music-hall audience. Following this, press interest in "Bouncing Bertha" began to wane.

There was, however, still some academic interest in the case. Two professors from the University of Tennessee—Dr. George Haslerud and Dr. Axel Brett, both leaders in the field of philosophy and psychology—decided to investigate further. Dr. Brett, who had made a study of the spasmodic ecstatic worship of "holiness religions" in Tennessee, was particularly intrigued by Bertha's case. The two men visited the Sybert cabin to observe and take measurements of the alleged haunting. Whist they were there, the spectre became particularly boisterous. According to the *Spartanburg Herald,* sausages jumped around the academics' dinner plates, and a tureen of soup mysteriously upended itself. Initially Brett refused to discuss his findings, simply stating that they were "peculiar" without giving any further clarification. Later both he and Dr. Haslerud stated that they had noticed "unusual and noticeable bodily contractions" in relation to Bertha.

These, they deduced, were the voluntary (or, more likely, involuntary) source of the bouncing. Their statements also implied that the family might have exaggerated the symptoms for some unknown reason, perhaps in order to gain fame or financial recompense from the press.

Most people in the Blue Ridge area dismissed these findings. Tourists and sightseers still made their way up to Wallens Creek in the hopes of seeing Bertha or even the poltergeist activity for themselves. Other entertainment promoters put the phenomenon down to skilled acrobatics and wanted to hire her. All of this suggested that many people outside the immediate area now thought that the phenomena were self-manufactured and had little to do with the supernatural. As interest and speculation began to fade, the eerie incidents appeared to become more sporadic, as well. Roughly three months after it had begun, the bouncing suddenly and inexplicably came to an end. Whatever unquiet spirits had been troubling Bertha were now completely gone, and whatever terrors she had experienced were quickly pushed to the back of her mind. Gradually her name faded from general memory. Bertha Sybert grew up, married, and raised a family without ever experiencing this kind of supernatural event again. In her latter years she was badly troubled by arthritis, which virtually crippled her. She died in Surry County, Virginia, in 1986 at the age of 57, without ever experiencing anything mysterious again. Nor, like Laura, did she ever speak of the strange experiences that had so blighted her early years.

So what was it that had tormented Bertha Sybert? Was it something that had lurked in the Blue Ridge since before the Native Americans came? Was it "witchy magic," as Grandma Jane Sybert, standing at the door of her cabin, had hinted? Or was it, as the Tennessee academics had suggested, some form of either voluntary or involuntary hoax? Could it be that Bertha was simply a fairly skilled acrobat who, under certain conditions, could perform tricks that terrified her immediate family and friends? When she was placed in a controlled environment with observers, such as in a Vaudeville theatre in front of an audience, the phenomena did not occur. Or could it be that, as it was in Laura's case, there was some form of repressed emotion involved that found itself contained in a rigid family and community setting, and which was augmented by the onset of puberty, only to explode in a violent and alarming way? There may be no way of knowing the true answers to any of these questions, which is testament to the enduring and confounding nature of these poltergeist cases.

The Solicitor's Poltergeist

This particular instance of alleged poltergeist activity took place in Rosenheim, Southern Bavaria, Germany, in 1967, and had rather curious beginnings. The bizarre activities began not in some gloomy bedroom in an isolated farmhouse or cabin, but in the busy, modern offices of a German solicitor. Despite the somewhat prosaic surroundings, however, there seemed to be an element of emotional or sexual repression in this case, too.

Sigmund Adam ran a successful legal business near the center of the city, employing a number of staff, several of whom were engaged in the day-to-day operations of his offices. Around the latter half of 1967, a series of odd events began to occur, beginning with the internal telephone network. Phones rang continually but when they were answered no-one spoke, although staff later indicated that they intuited a presence on the other end of the line. Convinced that his company was the victim of a persistent prank caller, Adam reported the matter to the authorities. Things took a more serious turn when the firm received its quarterly telephone bill. The initial account detailed 46 calls to the German-speaking clock (number 0119) in a 10-minute period. Even more convinced that he was the

victim of a trick—perhaps even from one of his own employees—
Adam once again contacted the telephone company, Deutsche Post,
who then installed monitoring equipment as well as a telephone lock
which only Adam himself could open. Nevertheless, the calls to the
speaking clock continued; during a period of five weeks the equipment registered an amazing 600 calls within 15-minute intervals,
faster than any human hand could dial (remember that in those
days there was only the rotary phone). Other strange things began
to occur around the office. Lights switched themselves on and off;
photocopiers inexplicably gushed fluid; and desk and cabinet draw-
ers opened and closed without anyone touching them. The mysterious calls continued at an even greater frequency.

Still convinced that there was some sort of rational explanation, the police and the telephone and power companies investigated but found nothing. One interesting fact did emerge, though:
through a series of clandestine recording footage, both visual
and audio, it soon became evident that the disruptions only occurred when a 19-year-old secretary, Anne-Marie Schneider, was
in the building. Anne-Marie, a recent hire, was a rather troubled
individual. Her surname is sometimes given as Scabari, a name
which she may have used to create another and perhaps more
romantic identity for herself. She was a rather preoccupied individual who, during the previous few years, had gone through a
number of disappointing dating relationships. Many in the office
suspected that the strange activities might have something to do
with her, but nothing was proven either way.

Still convinced that there was some fault in the telephone and
electrical systems, Adam had the power company set up more
monitoring equipment within the offices. This new effort revealed
something startling. Incredibly, there was a tremendous power
surge every time Anne-Marie entered the building. The electrical voltage rose to levels so high that, ordinarily, they would have

blown every fuse in the breaker box. But no fuses blew. Film footage also showed that a number of overhead lights seemed to flicker when she passed beneath them; one even appeared to swing dangerously on its cord as she walked by. In an attempt to isolate the problem, the firm closed down all main power and switched to a stand-by generator, but the fluctuations still continued whenever Anne-Marie was in the building.

Things came to a critical head in October of 1967. Lights began rotating in their sockets and photocopiers began to operate by themselves, turning out sheets of blank paper. A heavy cupboard allegedly moved several feet without leaving a mark on the floor. Early in 1968, pages on a calendar were ripped off by unseen forces and pictures were turned around so that they were facing the wall. Word had begun to leak out about the strange events, which by then were thought to be the result of a bona fide poltergeist. Dr. Hans Bender, a well-known German parapsychologist from the Freiberg Institute, and two scientists from the Max Planck Institute decided to conduct a number of tests on the so-called poltergeist and on Anne-Marie herself. They filmed the lights, which seemed to turn when she walked past them, and made several recordings of the energy levels, which seemed to fluctuate when she was in the room. When Bender interviewed Anne-Marie, he found her to be rather immature for her age and prone to moodiness and depression. The breakup of her last relationship had traumatized her to the extent that Bender thought she might be suffering from some kind of mild neurosis. Significantly, he also discovered that she loathed her work and had a deep-seated, almost vitriolic dislike for her employer. It was also noted that when she went on vacation, the bizarre activities ceased. Bender came to the conclusion that the girl's repressed feelings of grief (over the failed relationships) and rage (directed at her employer) were clearly linked to the extraordinary phenomena.

Although he did not fully agree with the assessment, Sigmund Adam decided that there might be indeed some connection and fired Anne-Marie, whereupon the disturbances ceased completely. She was subsequently employed by a couple of other firms, all of which experienced similar electrical anomalies but not to the same extent. According to some stories, she once got into a fight with a date at a bowling alley and caused the scoreboard to malfunction. By 1969, however, Anne-Marie Schneider had settled down and gotten married, and the poltergeist activity surrounding her had ceased. At this point, she vanishes from the pages of history.

The Rosenheim case was and still remains a controversial one. It has been suggested that Anne-Marie somehow engineered the eerie activity herself in order to annoy her employer. It's even been suggested that it was brought about by Sigmund Adam himself in order to gain some publicity for his business (his firm subsequently prospered, arguably as a result of the notoriety). Or could it be, as Bender hinted, that the intense, repressed emotions of an immature young woman had manifested themselves in strange and violent ways? That remains the core of the debate concerning the Rosenheim poltergeist—as well as many other cases like it—to this day.

Because of space limitations, I've only been able to provide limited details regarding three relatively straightforward instances of so-called poltergeist activity. There are, of course, many other more complex cases. Apart from the Articlave case, these "poltergeists" appear to be little more than the release of violent and often repressed energies and emotions. The entities or energies in other cases, such as that of "Corney" in 18th-century Dublin; the case of

Esther Cox in Amherst, Nova Scotia; or the events surrounding the Fox Sisters (the founders of modern-day Spiritualism) have spoken, written, or made their presence known in a relatively intelligent manner. Others still, such as the Drummer of Tedworth, have simply manifested themselves by making strange, inexplicable sounds. Some of these cases, of course, may well have been hoaxes perpetuated for various purposes. And yet, at the core of almost every poltergeist case there seems to lie a reciprocal relationship between the poltergeist and its victim or victims, whether the manifestation is that of a violent energy, strange voices, or mysterious writing. At present we are only beginning to understand some of the things that actually make us human—emotion, reason, pleasure, despair—and to recognize how powerful these things are. Is there a part of our body—somewhere in our brain, perhaps— that can act as a channel for that power and externalize it into our immediate surroundings in some tangible way? Based on the evidence in these three cases alone, it would certainly seem so. And yet, this solution or explanation poses even more questions than it answers. Does the source of such disruption lie solely within ourselves, or is there some part of us that can, whether consciously or unconsciously, animate a force that usually lies dormant within our surroundings, making it, in effect, a *genius loci*? Moreover, if the latter is true, are those forces stirred into some form of life by repressed emotions, particularly those of prepubescent or pubescent and perhaps immature girls or feelings of strong religious fervour (as perhaps was the case in Articlave)? Or is it brought into being by something else entirely? And finally, can such forces, once released, be controlled in any way?

Of course, there are many other explanations for the phenomenon. "Poltergeist" hauntings may indeed be ghosts trying to communicate, however inarticulately, with the living. What is clear, however, is that rather than concentrating on more sensational, individual cases, the problem needs to be studied as a whole in both historical and, as far as it is possible, scientific terms. Maybe only then can we truly discover what a poltergeist actually is.

Bibliography

Ackroyd, Peter. *The English Ghost*. London: Chatto and Windus, 2010.

Brennan, K. *Passing Strange: Eerie Stories from Ireland*. London: Bosworth, 1939.

Bynum, Joyce. "Poltergeists—A Phenomenon Worthy of Serious Study." In *A Review of General Semantics*. Fort Worth, Tex.: Institute of General Semantics Summer, 1993.

Crowe, Catherine. *The Night Side of Nature or Ghosts and Ghost Seers*. London: George Routledge and Sons Ltd., 1847.

Curran, Bob. "Bouncing Bertha." In *Mysterious Celtic Mythology in American Folklore*. Gretna, La.: Pelican Publishing, 2010.

Fodor, Nandor and H. Carrington. *Haunted People: The Story of the Poltergeist Down the Centuries*. London: Dutton, 1951.

Fodor, Nandor. *On the Trail of the Poltergeist*. New York: Citadel Press, 1958.

Gauld, Alan and A.D. Cornell. *Poltergeists*. London: Routledge and Kegan Paul, 1979.

LaChance, Steven. *The Uninvited*. Woodbury, Minn.: Llewellyn, 2009.

Keenan, B.T. *Seen at Dusk: A Collection of Irish Phantoms*. Dublin: Windsor Press, 1947.

Kelly, Lynne. *The Skeptic's Guide to the Paranormal*. London: Allen and Unwin, 2004.

Playfair, G.N. *The Indefinite Boundary: An Investigation into the Relationship Between Matter and Spirit*. London: Souvenir Press, 1976.

Thurston, H. *Ghosts and Poltergeists*. London: Burns, Oates and Washbourne, 1953.

Wilson, Colin. *Poltergeist*. Woodbury, Minn.: Llewellyn, 1993.

The Immortals: Understanding Apparitions

By Joshua P. Warren

Have you ever seen a ghost? Do you *want* to see one? When some people talk about ghosts, they mean a swirl of mist on a cold night or a glowing sphere that sweeps through a darkened room. The kind of ghost I'm talking about is the kind that stops you in your tracks: a fully formed, distinct person suddenly standing right in front of you. It's the kind of thing that shoots a bolt of terror down your spine. One minute you're alone, and the next, someone else is there—someone who is not in the world of the living. The fear can be almost painful. It is unreal, incongruous, primordially eerie. Who is this person? What is this thing? Why are you seeing it? That is where we must begin.

On September 11, 2001, the world cried out when more than 3,000 people died on American soil. Imagine the pain if that number had been more than 600,000—for that is how many perished during four years of the American Civil War. In just one battle, at Cold Harbor, Virginia, at least 7,000 men were slaughtered in only 20 minutes. From April 1861 to April 1865, the United States was truly transformed into hell on earth. Women who lost loved ones, especially a husband, would customarily dress in black for a year or more. In the state of Alabama alone, there were more than 80,000 widows. The streets of America were filled with mourning women, quietly drifting along like dark, lost phantoms, with veils covering their numb, empty faces. The entire country was a ghost town in every sense of the word, filled with death and suffering, a swirling, dismal landscape of miserable human energy. One of the worst places of all, where stinking creeks ran red with blood and towering layers of dismembered corpses filled the horizon, was the battlefield at Gettysburg, Pennsylvania.

In May of 2001, during Memorial Day weekend (just months before September 11), a great historian and ghost investigator spent an evening at Gettysburg. His name is Patrick K. Burke, and he is president of the American Battlefield Ghost Hunters Society (*www.TrentHallMedia.com*). Accompanied by a handful of associates, he quietly and respectfully observed the uneasy calm at an especially terrible site: the Triangle Field. There, on July 2 of 1863, Southern General James Longstreet's corps of soldiers crept toward a cursed spot called Devil's Den. According to acclaimed Civil War expert Dr. William R. Forstchen, they suffered terrible casualties. It was one of the most violent days in an unimaginably gory battle.

Burke scanned the dark field with his Sony video camera, using the Night Shot feature to pull detail from the night. This setting makes the video sensitive to infrared light, which is usually invisible to the naked eye. The camera shines an infrared illuminator, which acts like a flashlight for the video processor, thus revealing the surroundings to the person holding the camera. In front of Burke, a tourist with his head hung thoughtfully walked in front of the camera. There was a shallow rim of risen earth there that had once been a low wall during the actual fighting, 138 years earlier. The man's shirt glowed brightly, reflecting the infrared beam just as it should. But in front of the man, materializing in a fleeting wisp, seemingly from nowhere out of the dark, appeared something shocking. Burke didn't actually see it until he played back the tape and analyzed it later.

Just a few steps in front of the tourist appeared what looked like another man. However, the second figure was not a physical form at all. As you can see in the first frame of Burke's video, the mysterious second figure does not reflect the infrared illuminator; instead, he appears translucent, as if the light were simply passing through him.

The bright figure on the left is a real man. However, the translucent figure on the right is an apparition. The specter seems to be lifting his leg over a low wall that no longer exists, but which did actually exist during the Civil War. Photo courtesy Patrick K. Burke, *www.TrentHallMedia.com.*

Dressed in a soldier's cap and coat, the figure marches steadfastly forward, looking straight ahead. And, perhaps most amazingly, his right leg is bent back, as if he were dragging it over the wall that used to be there 138 years ago. The effect is enhanced by the clear 90-degree bend in the knee. The second and third frames clearly show his next two steps, as the partially visible "soldier" slips out of view and, perhaps, back into the ether.

Top, the apparition appears to be stepping solidly on the ground, looking straight ahead. *Bottom,* the apparition quickly moving forward, intently focused on something ahead of him. Photos courtesy Patrick K. Burke, *www.TrentHallMedia.com.*

It appears that Burke managed to capture on video a classic full-bodied apparition in motion, at a location saturated in a tragic and bloody history. "I had three other people with me," he said. "I asked each person [who] was there with me what they saw when I was shooting.... Each person said they saw the one man.... Each person clearly indicated that there was no other person in front of, or next to him, at the time I filmed him." And yet, plainly visible on the infrared-sensitive footage, was a figure out of place and time. This apparition was interacting with a landscape from long ago, not the one present in 2001. It's like a recording trapped in time. We call this an *imprint*. More on that later.

Ironically, before I had even learned of Burke's video, a friend and fellow investigator from North Carolina shared his own amazing experience with me. Richard Liebeck also knew nothing of Burke's footage. However, on Sunday, July 22, 2007, he, too, was in the Triangle Field to research the paranormal. The only other person present was his brother, Randy, who stood at his side. Around 5 p.m., they suddenly started picking up weird electromagnetic fluctuations on a Tri-Field Natural EM Meter, which is an uncommon occurrence in the middle of an open field. An avid photographer, Richard lifted his digital Kodak DX7590 and started shooting the sunny field. At first, all seemed normal.

He took a clear shot of an old foot path, but it was his next photos that triggered his curiosity. A part of the path looked a bit hazy, as if the light were being refracted slightly; the effect was similar to the way heat waves rise from a hot roadway (*overleaf*).

Here is a clear shot of the narrow footpath in front of Richard Liebeck.
(Photo courtesy Richard Liebeck, *www.BlueRidgeParanormal.com*.)

Since it was a bright and sunny day, he wondered what would happen if he blocked the light by using a Hoya R72 infrared filter. (These filters look like circles of opaque black glass.) Only infrared light above 720 nm makes it into the camera. All digital cameras are somewhat sensitive to infrared light; you can see this by pointing a digital camera at a TV remote and hitting a button on the remote—a light will emanate that can only be seen through the camera.

With the infrared filter screwed onto his lens, Richard took another shot of the empty field. The monochromatic image was difficult to see on a LCD screen (*opposite*):

During broad daylight, Liebeck took this photo of the field using an infrared filter, only allowing frequencies invisible to the human eye to pass through into the camera. Though no physical form was in front of him, note the dark figure standing to the right. (Photo courtesy Richard Liebeck, *www.BlueRidgeParanormal.com*.)

Later, however, when he viewed it on a computer, his jaw hit the floor. Though he hadn't seen a single soul in front of him when he snapped the photo, he could clearly see the stark figure of a man standing on the path, directly facing him. It was even clearer when magnified and enhanced in black and white. A chill ran down his spine as he gazed at the ghostly image (*overleaf*):

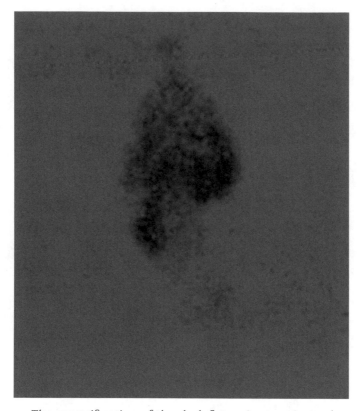

The magnification of the dark figure is stunning to behold. It appears to be a spectral soldier, holding his rifle
and staring directly into the camera.
(Photo courtesy Richard Liebeck,
www.BlueRidgeParanormal com.)

I showed the photo to Dr. William R. Forstchen during a live radio show I host, and recorded his reaction. I'd never seen the good
doctor's expression register such surprise. He looked as if...well, as
if he'd seen a ghost. His analysis was startling: "What I'm looking
at," he said, "is someone in a kepi [a soldier's cap]. I can detect
faint crosshatching, which would be straps for [the] cartridge box
and haversack. Under his left arm is a large bulge, which is usually
the hip that you wore your haversack on, which contained your ra-
tions and such." He paused, fully absorbed the image, shook his

head and sighed in awe. "You've got something in this photograph. There's something there."

"So," I replied, "based upon the obvious appearance, it looks as though this could represent the actual supplies and uniform that an authentic soldier of that era would have had?"

Forstchen was resolute. "This looks like a soldier in uniform," he stated confidently. "*Definitely*. Definitely—it's a soldier in uniform." From a history professor specializing in the Civil War and a *New York Times* best-selling author who has published more than 50 books, these were powerful words.

Although they may seem similar, the soldier in Richard Liebeck's photo is fundamentally different from the one in Burke's footage. Liebeck's soldier is standing directly on the present-day pathway. Though the foot trail (or something like it) may have existed 144 years ago, it's doubtful that it would have been in that precise spot, possessing the same width and height, after so many decades of erosion. Furthermore, though Liebeck's soldier is off to the right of the shot, he appears to have his body turned toward the camera, as though he were staring straight at the photographer. As soon as you see it, you feel that the specter is eerily aware of the fact that it is being observed. You get the sense that he is sizing you up with his steady gaze. When a phantom exhibits an awareness of its present-day surroundings and seems to interact with them, it is called an *entity*. More on that later, as well.

In the two examples I've given so far, digital technology has been used to capture an image. Even though digital cameras are naturally somewhat sensitive to infrared, in both cases, that sensitivity was enhanced even further with the use of a special setting or filter. Such modifications may increase your odds of seeing and recording such an apparition, but they're not essential. Throughout history, some of the most interesting full-bodied apparitions have

This photo shows the massive construction underway during the White House renovation in 1950. (Photo courtesy U.S. National Parks Service.)

been captured using standard mechanical cameras with no special films or filters geared toward infrared imagery. One of the more interesting examples of this that just recently came to light was taken in a truly grand and amazing place: the White House.

From 1949 to 1952, during the presidency of Harry S. Truman, the White House was undergoing major renovations. Much of the process was officially documented for the public by National Parks Service photographer Abbie Rowe. When David McCullough published his Pulitzer Prize–winning biography, *Truman*, it included some of Rowe's photos. In 2008, I was contacted by a fellow named Bob Martin; he was an extremely attentive reader of that book who had noticed a strange detail in one of Rowe's images.

A closer look at the photo shows a group of men in the background standing to the left. But there is also an odd, translucent figure, standing by itself to the right. (Photo courtesy U.S. National Parks Service.)

The photograph, taken around 1950, shows a rough, hulled out section of the White House during renovation.

The structure is stripped to bare bones—brick walls, dirt floor, and steel beams. In the foreground, a worker seated on a bulldozer seems to pause and pose for the camera, leaning heavily on one of his controls.

In the background and to the left, three men are standing in front of the back wall and near a tall post. All of that looks normal. But to the right of the three men and against the back wall (above the bulldozer driver's head) stands a lone figure. Though properly proportioned, it is a translucent ghost.

In the closeup (*overleaf*) you can clearly see the figure standing erect and poised at attention, with his legs solidly apart and his

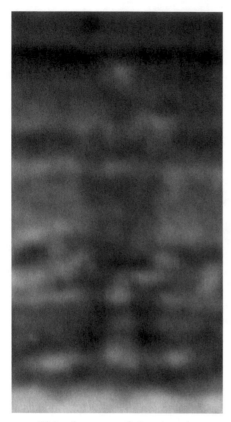

This close-up of the translucent figure clearly shows the eerie, mirage-like body. (Photo courtesy U.S. National Parks Service.)

hands folded in front. The shape of the head indicates that he is either wearing a hat of some sort or standing in profile, with his face looking up and to the left. The patterns of the wall behind him are distinctly visible through his mirage-like form.

Some photographic experts have wondered if this ghost could simply be the product of a protracted exposure time. But this explanation doesn't make sense. Everything else in the photo, including the three men next to him, is remarkably clear. And even if this were the imprint of a man who was running from the frame, there should have been some blurring around him. His form, though transparent, is quite sharply delineated. It is a remarkably weird image that conjures up many possibilities, particularly in a place as historic as the White House. It's difficult to say whether this is an imprint or an actual entity. The back wall in the photo had presumably been there for at least 150 years before the photo was taken, and many other men must have surely stood with their backs to it at one time or another. Perhaps it was once part of the closely guarded basement area. Or perhaps a curious spirit had showed up to observe the work in progress. Some researchers have noted that the figure resembles a bearded Abraham Lincoln—a well-known phantom in the White House—wearing a coat and peering up and to his left. This picture, along with the Burke footage and Liebeck photo, will give you a good idea of the three basic ways in which full-bodied apparitions can appear on various visual media.

Entities and Imprints

Before we dig into what these specters are and how they manifest in the physical world, let's address the issue that causes the most confusion: the difference between entities and imprints. Have you ever been to a wax museum? If you've ever visited Madame Tussaud's, famous for its uncanny reproductions of celebrities, you probably have photos of yourself standing next to the famous wax figures. If you stroll through the museum you often see tourists posing next to the wax forms. At first glance, the tourists and the figures appear the same—but they are not. Some are sentient human beings, while some are simply waxen 3-D representations of the real thing. In this sense, the tourists are similar to entities, while the wax figures are similar to imprints. Outwardly, both look the same, but only one possesses true consciousness. We can approximate the real thing using wax or some other medium, but we cannot re-create organic, intelligent awareness, despite our best efforts right now with AI (artificial intelligence).

Let's take this analogy one step further. Instead of wax figures standing in a static pose, imagine if they moved like the animatronic U.S. presidents at Disney World. The presidents speak and gesture, but they are limited to doing only what has been programmed into them. They have no free will or ability to choose. They are locked into a set destiny, replaying the same presentation over and over for each new audience. No matter how closely they seem to emulate a living person, they are not alive. In the same fashion, imprints are similar to life-size 3-D movies from the past that replay under certain conditions or for certain observers on the holographic "movie screen" of space-time. They are recordings, no different, really, than complex electrical signals on a videotape. But the beings that slip in and out of our dimensions, that have consciousness, are the entities. Yet where does all this energy come from, and why is it there in the first place? To answer these questions, we must examine life itself.

Life is the most mysterious force of all. All matter is comprised of particles, and one might argue that all particles possess awareness to some degree—or at least exhibit some kind of sensitivity to their surroundings—as they are all in a constant state of movement at the most microscopic level. But when we use ourselves as the point of comparison, we're looking for a particular type of life. Perhaps the most basic example is the amoeba. An amoeba is essentially a diaphanous bubble of slime, with no brain and no nervous system, and certainly no nose, eyes, mouth, or ears. And yet we know that it is alive in some sense. Amoebas are clearly aware of their surroundings—they prefer a certain water temperature and salinity over others, they interact with each other, and they hunt for food. What is this force that fills these creatures with life? We look inside them with our most powerful microscopes, yet we cannot see this force. However, the energy inside, the supreme animating force called life, is crudely expressed in the amoeba's activities. This force somehow connects with and animates the part we can see. We tend to see the mind (consciousness) and matter (the physical body) as two separate things, but perhaps they are really two sides of the same coin. Perhaps the mind and body are just different, ever-changing frequencies of the same impulse or primary force.

Whatever the case, the force that animates the single cell of an amoeba is no more or less enigmatic than what animates our own bodies. Whether it's one cell or trillions of cells working in unison, life finds form in an outward expression, and that expression changes each moment. You were once a small baby, but your outward form has morphed and grown. We define ourselves most easily at the physical level—the most apparent boundary, our fleshly bodies. However, our energy, our life force, doesn't stop at the boundary of our skin; it actually extends into a shell-like layer of distinct electrical and magnetic charges. In fact, I would argue that it is this layer of electromagnetic energy around us that contains our life and soul. This idea is exemplified by the work of a physicist at Cuza University in Romania, as reported in *New Scientist* in September of 2003.

Professor Mircea Sanduloviciu and his colleagues re-created the dynamic conditions they believe existed on our planet billions of years ago. This included passing powerful bolts of electricity similar to lightning through a highly energized mix of gases such as argon. They were amazed to watch cell-like spheres of plasma appear in microseconds, some of them as large as one inch in diameter. After self-organizing and forming distinct boundaries and an inner nucleus, these "cells" took on surprisingly life-like qualities. They could replicate, grow, replenish themselves, even "communicate" with each other by emitting electromagnetic energy, making the atoms within other spheres vibrate at a particular frequency. Sanduloviciu thinks these spheres may have been what the first cells on earth looked like, saying, "The emergence of such spheres seems likely to be a prerequisite for biochemical evolution."[1]

If it is true that life is first and foremost an electrical impulse or field, such as the energy fields referenced by Professor Sanduloviciu, the physical part of the body, the part we usually fixate on, is certainly misleading. After all, plants do not possess a body per se, yet they still qualify as living things. Everything that is alive has an *electromagnetic* body. Once you shift your paradigm to accommodate this fact, many of the mysteries surrounding full-bodied apparitions, and paranormal activity in general, become a bit more understandable. But it is the question of just how powerful the human field is, and to what extent it can exist and function independent of the body, that usually consumes our thoughts and attention.

The Bio-Energy Field

I am the founder and director of a research team and lab called L.E.M.U.R. (League of Energy Materialization and Unexplained Phenomena Research). We've been active since 1995, and are proud to have made the cover of a science journal, *Electric Spacecraft*, in 2004, for our groundbreaking work on understanding plasma physics in nature, in our study of the elusive Brown Mountain Lights. Our L.E.M.U.R. lab is not slick and fancy—it was cobbled together independently throughout the years from a variety of sources— and yet it's full of passionate people, new ideas, and creative ways of testing those ideas. In fact, I believe we're the first group that can adapt almost any paranormal or esoteric subject into a testable experiment. Much of our focus has been the mind-body-environment relationship.

For years, one prominent topic of our research has been people who focus on manipulating the body's energy field. Some of the more interesting subjects have been martial artists. In particular, Grandmaster Tom Cameron, of Chicago, Illinois, caught our attention long ago. He's one of the world's few publicly accessible practitioners of Dim Mak, the Chinese "death touch," and founder of his own discipline, Shin Be Han. Cameron has appeared on many TV programs (*Ripley's* called him the "human stun gun"); he's most famous for his controversial demonstrations in which he apparently knocks people down from several feet away without any physical contact. Cameron focuses his energy then blasts it forth with a violent thrust of his hands and a chesty yell.

I was present for one demonstration that was aired on the History Channel's *Stan Lee's Superhumans* in 2010. A doctor and EMTs confirmed that one subject who had been remotely knocked down by Cameron suffered a distinct drop in blood pressure that could not be medically explained, hypnotically induced, or faked. On numerous occasions through the years, our team has recorded bizarre electronic failures and inexplicable surges of electrical energy when Cameron projects his chi. The results have been inconsistent, however, so we have reached no solid conclusions. But one of our most intriguing experiments, in 2010, may have given us an intimate glimpse into how the human bio-energy field connects with the physical body.

One of our L.E.M.U.R. researchers, Big Joe Southards, at a strapping 6 feet 4 inches and 265 pounds, volunteered to be knocked out by Cameron for a test. Before the test, Joe placed his finger into the light-sealed pouch of a Kirlian camera that I was operating. Kirlian cameras pass a current of electricity—in this case, 5,000 volts at low amperage—through the human body and onto the film. This creates a direct image of the electrical energy that passes through the body. The subtle field of energy surrounding the body that is typically not able to be captured on film is energized enough to actually create an image. It's a fascinating way of glimpsing the energy surrounding our bodies. We took a control photo of Joe's fingertip while he stood calmly at rest. As you can see, a typical ring of light, called a *corona*, appears around the point of contact (*overleaf, top*).

Next, Cameron asked Joe to clench his teeth. Once everyone was ready, Cameron projected his energy and gave Joe a light tap on a pressure point near his jaw. At the precise moment the tap was delivered, I exposed the Kirlian film. Though the tap appeared harmless, Big Joe saw stars and fell backward, just as expected, and was safely lowered into a chair by fellow researcher Dean

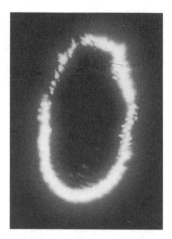

A control Kirlian photo of Joe Southard's fingertip shows a typical, singular coronal ring. (Photo by the author.)

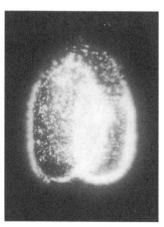

Another Kirlian photo of Joe Southard's fingertip, taken as Cameron tapped Joe with a chi projection, shows a weird double-corona. (Photo by the author.)

Warsing. What the second Kirlian photo (*bottom*) showed was amazing. This time, instead of one ring of light emanating from Joe's fingertip, there were *two* overlapping rings of light.

Keep in mind that the second photo was exposed for only a split second. The camera is designed so that voltage is being delivered throughout the entire exposure time. Therefore, if this effect were simply the product of Joe's motion, there would have been a blur—a smear of light across the film. Instead, each ringed image is absolutely, clearly intact, right down to the fingerprint ridges. I have taken thousands of Kirlian photos throughout the years, but I had never seen this before. It almost looked like a double exposure, but it was not. So what in the world had we captured?

In my opinion, one of the rings shows the bio-electricity around Joe's body. The other ring shows that his energy body had nearly separated from his physical body at the instant he almost lost consciousness. If he had gone under completely or even died, and we were able to photograph that at that precise moment, we may have actually seen two completely separated rings instead of two overlapping ones. What we probably captured was a glimpse of

Joe's full-bodied apparition! It retained the structure and design of his physical form, but, as you can see, it was not permanently attached. If we could have taken a Kirlian photo of his entire body at the time, I suspect we would have seen his entire apparition just slightly removed, or knocked askew, from his physical body. I know a man who claims he was literally knocked completely out of his body for a few moments after he was hit in the face with a baseball. Amazingly, he claims that his awareness and sentience stayed with the *energy* that was released, not with his body!

This was a profound discovery, and right in keeping with what we already knew about the human body. The electrostatic field around you can pack many thousands of volts. If we know that some fields are powerful enough to effect others physically, perhaps as Cameron's can, and that bio-fields can even leave the body, this gives us an enlightened view of full-bodied apparitions. We are talking about a powerful electrical field that matches the contours of the fleshy form but which can indeed separate and perhaps even carry our awareness with it—a subject we'll get back to shortly. But first, let's take a closer look at just what these energy forms can do in the physical world.

Electrostatic force

In our experiments, and especially in our lab, we have reproduced many of the effects associated with ghosts by using directed electrical energy. Concentrated electrostatic fields alone can accomplish most of the work. Remember those silver balls from high school science demonstrations that make your hair stand on end? They are called *Van de Graaff generators*. They work rather simply. A belt inside the device runs over two spindles, building up an electrical charge (the product of electrons being imbalanced as they are rubbed from one element to another). A small charge is collected by the metal dome, where it builds into a larger charge. Once the dome has reached its maximum capacity, a powerful bolt of electricity shoots out. When someone touches the dome, he or she becomes an extension of it. As the charge builds up in a person's body, the scalp and hair take on the same charge (usually positive, in this case). Because like charges repel, just as the same poles of two different magnets push apart from each other, the hair pushes away from the scalp. Time and time again, we hear stories about a someone's hair standing on end when they've encountered a spirit. This kind of electromagnetic effect could explain why.

As for the PK effects that are sometimes observed in haunting and poltergeist cases, by using these same concepts, we can easily move objects from a distance. By attaching a wire to a Van de Graaff generator, we can "spray" the charged particles in an "ion wind," in much the same way that pressure shoots water from a hose. Small items such as cigarettes or ping-pong balls roll easily across a table when a flow of ions is pointed toward them, even from several feet away. When it's directed at someone's back, it feels very much like a physical touch. In fact, it *is* a physical touch. That same flow of energy can create goose bumps and cold chills, and even cause nearby light bulbs to explode by overloading the filament. As well, fluorescent bulbs will blink on and off and even increase in brightness, whether they are plugged in or not, when they are held near such charges. Again, these are the same types of phenomena that are often reported during spectral close encounters.

In popular culture, the word "ghost" usually denotes something non-physical, something vague and ethereal that passes through walls. It is erroneous to think of ghosts as intangible things, however. The reality is that there is really no such thing as the non-physical, just different *levels* of physicality. Two different things resist

each other, and are therefore "physical to" each other, if they resonate within a similar frequency range. You can pick up a cup because both you and the cup occupy the same narrow slice of the
frequency spectrum. But you cannot feel radio waves, though your
body is most likely being bombarded by them right now. This is
because you and the waves are resonating at very different rates.
Nonetheless, a device specially tuned to interact with them (a radio) can turn their energy into sound, allowing you to enjoy a song
as you cruise down the highway. Ghosts appear as more or less
physical depending on these varying relationships. It's also why
one person will be able to perceive and interact with a particular
phantom, while another person will not. Therein lies the challenge
of dissecting the individual human experience. Based on the photos you've just seen, and based on my archive of similar results,
most ghosts seem to be more visible in the infrared frequency, a
slightly lower frequency than what our eyes can usually detect.
Who knows what we'll find when ultraviolet digital cameras become commonplace in the market?

Apparitions are fluctuations of energy that contain information. If you ask "Where is the spirit world?" you may as well ask
"Where is the Internet?" It isn't really a place, but rather an ex-
change of information that takes on somewhat malleable forms
in the electromagnetic (or as some metaphysicians call it, the
"etheric") medium around us. I once interviewed a brilliant scientist who said that cavemen would likely crack open a television set in order to find the little people inside. Of course, there
are no little people, just wires and components bearing no re-
semblance to a person at all. The people on the screen are organized patterns of energy, and require a human observer to
give them shape, context, and meaning. Imagine, then, that we
ourselves are similar to those little people on the screen, but to
our own scale. Yet our "set" is a much grander, more complex,

more holographic—or, as I call it, the *holosentient*—world. By "holosentient" I mean that the real world extends beyond the visual alone, and includes sounds, tastes, smells, and feelings. In fact, the worlds of TV and the Internet are but miniature, limited versions modeled on the grand one in which we live our lives. And so, what happens when we die? How do we become those full-bodied apparitions glimpsed or captured on film almost every day around the world?

Quantum Effects in Your Daily Life

First, we know from quantum physics that time is a flexible thing. It passes at different rates in relationship to the observer. On some level, the past to you is the future to someone else in the universe, and vice versa. Therefore, every single moment you exist you leave an imprint of yourself. In fact, your life is a continuous wave—a continuum of energy, if you will. Some moments stand out more strongly than others, though, especially at times when you exude extreme emotional energy. These moments create an imprint. It can be a split second—a still shot—or a short clip, like 20 seconds from a movie. During moments such as these, all around you is "drenched" with your energy and immersed in your expansive aura. Your clothes, nearby objects, even the ground you walk on are supercharged. The frequency of that unique imprint will resonate with people who are able to tune in to it, or with devices that are tuned to capture and measure it—a rare happenstance. Environmental conditions, such as temperature and humidity or even geomagnetic and solar cycles, will also affect how easily these subtle impressions present themselves.

Imprints also enable us to observe what appear to be two separate points in space-time simultaneously. For example, let's say we have a single fish swimming in a fish tank. We choose to observe this fish using two different video cameras. One camera is set up pointed straight at the face of the tank, and the other is pointed straight toward the side of the tank, perpendicular to the first camera. The images from both cameras are sent to another room. In that room are two monitors mounted side-by-side. A person watching the monitors who is unaware of the setup may assume he is looking at two different fish. However, he will quickly realize that when Fish 1 moves, Fish 2 moves at the exact same moment. It might be easy to assume that there is some invisible, non-linear connection between the two fish. A physicist might scratch her head and work out long calculations in attempt to explain this strange, seemingly non-local phenomenon. How is it that the two fish move instantaneously in tandem without being connected? Scientists are puzzled by this kind of behavior in particles all the time. In the same fashion, when we are viewing an imprint, perhaps we are actually seeing one manifestation of two different perspectives. Perhaps those visions of the past are not as distant as we assume them to be.

In order to understand entities, we need to consider the nature of awareness itself. Right now, your mind controls your body. If you decide to flex and raise your arm, the arm obeys. This is puzzling, because Newtonian physics stresses that action is necessary for reaction. Yet when we look for the source of the movement—thought itself—we cannot locate it. It appears there is a reaction without an action. This seems to indicate that thought, however we define it, is actually a force of physical power. If we know the body is much more than just matter, we must accept that our thoughts are connected to the energy body, as well. Because that energy body is capable of separating from the flesh, your mind, to some extent, travels with it. There is no "life after death," but simply a continuation of life. Because the mind controls the body, the mind may also control how the body appears. Hence, if your disembodied awareness wants to move about as a ball of light, so be it. Or if it wants to emulate how you looked at the age of 10, that's fine, too. It seems that entities can control how they appear to some extent, hence their ability to slip in and out of the physical plane. Generally speaking, the most well-defined full-bodied apparitions are probably the youngest (meaning they have been out of the physical flesh for less than a few hundred years). They probably undergo a period of adjustment before they can be comfortable changing appearance. And, of course, the shape that once adhered to the lines of flesh may also gradually break down into a more nebulous form, similar to the way a sandy hill slowly erodes when a retaining wall is removed.

Another intriguing aspect of these full-bodied entities can be found in new developments of quantum physics. In a fascinating article titled "Quantum Trickery: Testing Einstein's Strangest Theory" that appeared in the *New York Times* in December of 2005, physicists at the National Institute of Standards and Technology in Boulder, Colorado, were able to make atoms spin in two different directions at the same time:

> These [half dozen beryllium] atoms were each spinning clockwise and counterclockwise at the same time. Moreover, like miniature Rockettes they were all doing whatever it was they were doing together, in perfect synchrony. Should one of them realize, like the cartoon character who runs off a cliff and doesn't fall until he looks down, that it is in a metaphysically untenable situation and decide to spin only one way, the rest would instantly fall in line, whether they were across a test tube or across the galaxy.

Physicists call this a "cat state":

No, they were not sprawled along a sunny window-sill. To a physicist, a "cat state" is the condition of being two diametrically opposed conditions at once, like black and white, up and down, or dead and alive.[2]

Dead *and* alive? Could it be that we all exist in a kind of "cat state"? Is it possible that full-bodied entities don't realize that they're dead? We are seeing Liebeck's soldier and looking back 144 years. But, to that soldier, is it still the day of the battle? How has time changed for both of us? Is it possible that right now, as you read these very words, you are, yourself—dare I say it—dead? I'm willing to bet you are. We all are, but we are experiencing life one little moment at a time, and that will continue for eternity.

It was once believed that these oddball quantum effects only mattered on a scale too small for us to imagine. But all that changed in March of 2010. The esteemed publication *Nature* reported that scientists at the University of California–Santa Barbara had, for the first time, been able to put an object large enough to be seen with the naked eye (a metal paddle 30 micrometers long, just slightly bigger than a human hair) into a state of moving and not moving at once. "The experiment shows that the principles of quantum mechanics can apply to everyday objects as well as atomic-scale particles," reads the article.[3] This is earth-shattering news. It would seem that even the most bizarre and inexplicable aspects of our paranormal experiences are, in fact, common and quite easily explained, at least in the quantum realm.

Our Fate as Immortals

Our ability to grasp the mystery of full-bodied apparitions, and many other paranormal phenomena, will be contingent on the development of appropriate language. Thoughts follow words. If I told someone living in 1710 that "imprints are similar to electrical signals on a VHS tape," he would have no idea what I meant. I would first have to define my terms and demonstrate the basic concepts to give him a background understanding. Then, I would go on to explain how a VHS tape shows up on a TV, and so on. But now that we can talk about the Internet and cell phones, lasers and holograms, time travel and quantum physics, our minds can grow in leaps and bounds, with sources and resources only a few mouse clicks away. Collectively, our technology is speeding closer and closer to capturing a full explanation of mysteries that once seemed impossible to comprehend.

Whether imprints or entities, full-bodied apparitions are perhaps the starkest and most compelling examples of classic ghostly phenomena. Because they were once fully, physically human, just as we are, we can sometimes perceive them on rare occasions. They are clear information from another time and place, expressed in ways that can touch, illuminate, and even speak. Sometimes they terrify us, yet on those rare occasions when we interact with them, they remind us of something very important: The energy inside us never truly dies. All of us are immortal.

Notes

1. Cohen, David, "Plasma Forms Hint at New Form of Life," *New Scientist* online, September, 2003, *http://www.newscientist.com/article/dn4174-plasma-blobs-hint-at-new-form-of-life.html.*

2. Overbye, Dennis, "Quantum Trickery: Testing Einstein's Strangest Theory," The *New York Times* online, December 27, 2005, *http://www.nytimes.com/2005/12/27/science/27eins.html.*

3. Brumfiel, Geoff, "Scientists Supersize Quantum Mechanics," *Nature* online, March 17, 2010, *http://www.nature.com/news/2010/100317/full/news.2010.130.html.*

Talking to Ghosts

By Raymond Buckland

Most people have some sort of preconception of what a ghost is. Many carry the old Casper the Friendly Ghost image of a figure floating about in a sheet, while others have the Canterville Ghost in mind, a character from a past century that was transparent and walked through walls. The ghost of Hamlet's father; the ghosts of Christmas Past, Present, and Future from Charles Dickens's *A Christmas Carol*; Patrick Swayze's character in the movie *Ghost*—all of these have become stock representations of ghosts. But where do spirits fit in? What is the difference, if any, between a ghost and a spirit?

Although many hundreds of different forms and permutations of ghosts have been sighted all around the world, the majority of ghosts are, in fact, visual or audible forms of the spirits of the dead. They are people who have lived and died, and are returning in one form or another. Yet not all spirits of the dead choose to make themselves known or seen. So, while all ghosts are spirits, not all spirits are ghosts. To further explain this, we must examine what happens when we "cross over" or "transition." Now that I'm on the topic, there are many euphemisms for death, but in my opinion it's not just semantics. In the spirit (!) of calling a spade a spade, let's use the proper terminology.

The Spiritualist belief—which is actually held by millions of people, not just Spiritualists—is that when we die, our spirit passes on to the next level or plane, what I will call the Spirit World. There are various beliefs regarding what happens there, many that tie in with the idea of karma, for example. Whether or not we believe in reincarnation is irrelevant. For now, all that matters is that we acknowledge that at death, our spirit proceeds to this Spirit World. Many, if not most, spirits go there quite happily; others go kicking and screaming. For various reasons, many people are not all that happy at the prospect of having to leave the physical plane. They may feel that they have unfinished business; they may have died suddenly because of an accident, a murder, a sudden illness, or a natural disaster. Whatever the reason, they may feel (in so far as spirits are able to feel) that they need to stay on this plane until they have their affairs in order and are able to obtain some kind of closure. There are also the spirits who either cannot or will not acknowledge the fact that they have, in fact, died. These are the spirits who hang around, who become what we think of as ghosts. Again, not all spirits have a need to remain here; hence not all spirits are ghosts, but all ghosts are spirits.

The idea of ghosts is nothing new. The ancient Greeks fully accepted the idea of ghosts, as did the Romans. In Homer's *Odyssey*, for example, Odysseus encountered a warrior ghost when he wanted to cross into Hades. In ancient Greece, it was thought that the presence of a ghost meant that the person had not been given a proper burial. In the Middle Ages, the idea of ghosts was generally accepted, as well. Many attested to having seen the ghosts of Anne Boleyn and Catherine Howard, both wives of Henry VIII, not to mention the ghost of Henry himself. So ghosts have always been with us. But it was only in relatively recent times that we've been able to have *conversations* with ghosts.

Hydesville (sometimes spelled Hydeville) was a community in upstate New York that was founded by Dr. Henry Hyde in 1815. The area had been sparsely settled by pioneers 25 years previously, but Hyde constructed a small village there and named it for himself. One of the buildings he erected was a small, one-and-a-half-story weatherboard cabin built at the crossroads. Throughout the years it was occupied by a succession of families—first, Dr. Henry Hyde himself, and later, after his death, his son, Artemus Hyde. One family of renters was the Bells—John Bell and his wife, along with their 19-year-old maid, Lucretia Pulver. According to Lucretia's later testimony, a traveling peddler stopped by the cottage one evening to show his wares. The peddler carried with him a small tin trunk in which he kept his samples and all of his money. The Bells dismissed their maid shortly thereafter and sent her home. When she returned next morning there was no sign of the peddler and the Bells claimed that he had gone on his way. Mrs. Bell gave Lucretia a badly torn coat to repair, and during the next few days, showed off several silver thimbles and other items of the sort that a peddler might hock.

After the Bells vacated the cottage it was rented in 1846 to the Weekmans, along with their servant, Jane Lape. The Weekmans did not stay long, claiming that the house was haunted. In fact, Jane Lape claimed that she had seen a ghost and described it as wearing "grey pants, a black frock coat, and black cap."[1] Interestingly, Lucretia Pulver's earlier description of the peddler was that he was wearing a "black frock coat and light colored pants."[2] After they vacated the cottage, the Weekmans later complained that they had been constantly disturbed by all sorts of noises, including knocks and raps on the ceilings and walls.

In December of 1847, the Fox family—John and Margaret Fox, along with two of their daughters (Kate, 11, and Maggie, 14)—moved into the cottage. From the beginning of their tenancy there, they complained of similar noises. These increased in intensity and frequency to the point where, during the following spring, John Fox would insist on inspecting the building before the family retired for the night. He would ensure that all the shutters on the windows were tightly fastened, and not loose enough to be affected by any wind, and that no tree limbs were touching the outside of the house. He would also go from room to room, with candle in hand, inspecting the inside of the house for anything unusual or out of place. Yet despite these precautions, every night the family's sleep was interrupted with bangs and raps on ceilings and walls.

On the night of Friday, March 31, with all of them tired from the lack of sleep, the family retired early. In a later statement Mrs. Margaret Fox said:

> It was very early when we went to bed on this night—hardly dark. I had been so broken of rest I was almost sick.... I had just lain down. It commenced as usual. I knew it from all the other noises I had ever heard before. The children, who slept in the other bed in the room, heard the rapping, and tried to make similar sounds by snapping their fingers. My youngest child, Cathie [Kate], said "Mr. Splitfoot,[3] do as I do," clapping her hands. The sound instantly followed her with the same number of raps. When she stopped the sound ceased for a short time. Then Margaretta [Maggie] said, in sport, "No, do just as I do. Count one, two, three, four," striking one hand against the other at each time; and the raps came as before. She was afraid to repeat them.... I then thought I could put a test that no one in the place could answer. I asked the "noise" to rap my different children's ages successively. Instantly, each one of my children's ages was given correctly, pausing

between them sufficiently long to individualise them until the seventh, at which a longer pause was made, and then three more emphatic raps were given, corresponding to the age of the little one that died, which was my youngest child. I then asked: "Is this a human being that answers my questions so correctly?" There was no rap. I asked "Is it a spirit? If it is, give two raps." Two sounds were given as soon as the request was made.[4]

So Mrs. Fox was talking with the spirit—or, if you prefer, the ghost. Eventually, quite a few other people in that area of New York came forward and admitted that they had had similar experiences, but probably because their experiences were not as intrusive as those of the Fox family, they had done their best to ignore them. When word of the event spread, so did the fascination with spirit communication, thus starting the movement that was to develop into a worldwide religion. This was the beginning of modern Spiritualism, the practice of contacting and speaking to spirits.

In one of their conversations with the spirit, the Foxes learned that his name was Charles B. Rosna and that he had been murdered about five years prior to the Foxes coming into the home. This would put the event at about the time that the peddler disappeared while visiting the Bells. It wasn't until 1904 that his remains were discovered, along with his tin box, secreted in a wall in the basement of the cottage. The Bells were never charged with his murder, however, probably due to lack of concrete evidence tying the Bells to the crime.

So how were the Fox sisters able to communicate with this spirit or ghost of the peddler? Building on the simple yes-or-no answers and the counting, it wasn't long before the spirit was counting out the alphabet—one rap for A, two for B, three for C, and so on, in order to spell out long messages. This laborious form of communication was typical during the years following that initial connection. The Fox sisters eventually traveled around the area demonstrating their ability to communicate with the dead, but it meant many long hours going through the alphabet time and time again. Eventually table tipping came into vogue, which involved the spirit apparently tipping a small table onto two of its legs and then allowing it to fall back onto the floor when the correct letter of the alphabet was called out. Thus whole sentences could be spelled out, though it was still a very laborious process.

Today the media places a great deal of emphasis on "ghost hunting." Haunted places are invaded by the hunters, armed with cameras, EVP recorders, EMF meters, infrared thermometers, and the like. These modern tools can be excellent for determining that there is, in fact, a ghost or ghosts present, and even for obtaining recordings of ghostly sounds and voices. But lengthy conversations between a ghost and an investigator are still a rarity. For this, it seems that the old-fashioned methods may be best. Not necessarily the slow and laborious rapping and table tipping, but the later developments of the talking board and—by far the best method— automatic writing. A *séance* (the word simply means "sitting") conducted by a capable medium will, in all likelihood, give far more meaningful results than probing with a multitude of meters.

Today's mediums are able to connect directly with the spirits of the dead and see, hear, and/or sense what they have to say. There are two main varieties of mediumship: physical mediumship and mental mediumship. In the mental category there are subdivisions such as clairvoyance, clairaudience, clairsentience, and so on. *Clairvoyance* means "clear seeing," *clairaudience* is "clear hearing," and *clairsentience* is "clear sensing." This means that the medium is able to see, hear, and/or sense the spirit or ghost. Some mediums enjoy just one of these faculties, while others have two or all three of them. A medium, then, acts as a channel or conduit between the ghost and the living, thus eliminating the need for table-tipping or laborious counting.

Some mediums are even able to channel the actual voice of the deceased. This is known as *indirect voice*. When this happens, the spirit's voice comes through the medium's mouth; it usually sounds exactly like the deceased's did in life. There is also *independent voice*, which occurs when the voice comes not from the medium's mouth, but from a *trumpet* (a lightweight aluminum cone placed in the center of the séance table, or in the middle of the floor if there is no table) or from distant parts of the room. One such medium, and perhaps the most noteworthy, was Leslie Flint, an Englishman born in 1911. His first encounter with a ghost occurred when he was seven years old. An aunt's husband had been killed in World War I. When his aunt went to break the news to her mother (Flint's grandmother), Leslie saw the ghost of the dead man right there in the family kitchen with them. No one believed him, and yet only a few days later, he saw another ghost, this time of a neighbor who had been killed.

As a young man, Leslie Flint started attending Spiritualist churches and joined a *development circle*, a gathering of sitters (attendees) who wanted to learn how to become mediums. For a while nothing much happened—except when Leslie went to the local movie house, when he would invariably be shushed by the other patrons because of the voices that kept speaking out all around him. He was asked to leave the theater several times and eventually charged with creating a disturbance. One day, at one of his Spiritualist circles, he fell asleep; upon waking, he was told that he had spoken in several different voices—which turned out to be the voices of the other sitters' dead relatives. Soon he didn't have to fall asleep or go into trance to do this; he could simply sit with the others and the voices would come through him, unbidden.

What was especially unusual about Leslie Flint's channeling of spirit voices was that the sounds came not from his mouth but from his abdomen or, sometimes, from outside of his body, such as a far corner of the room. This was what was happening in the movie theatres. As word about his ability spread, he was typically accused of fraud. In response, Flint opened himself up to examination. He would often be tied in a chair, and his mouth and nose completely covered with tape, except for a tiny hole for him to breathe. The voices would still pour forth. And they were clear voices, both male and female. Sometimes the voices of famous deceased people would come through: Winston Churchill, Emily Brontë, Thomas Alva Edison, Maurice Chevalier, and others. Happily many of these examinations were recorded; the recordings are still extant, courtesy of the Leslie Flint Educational Trust. (You can listen to them on the Website, *www.leslieflint.com*). Flint worked tirelessly, without charging any money for what he did. He finally retired, and eventually died in Brighton in 1994 at the age of 83.

The majority of mediums are not as accomplished as Leslie Flint was, though many do channel the voices of spirits while in a trance. If a spirit's voice comes through a trumpet, the device will often float up into the air (luminous bands affixed to the ends allow this to be seen in the dark) and move about, thus amplifying the voices of the spirits when they speak. This is done through the medium insofar as energy is drawn from him or her, but there is no direct observable connection between the two. Because there is no physical connection, this phenomenon is classified under mental mediumship.

Similar phenomena have been reported by anthropologists conducting studies on indigenous tribal people. Waldemar Bogoras, an anthropologist studying the shamanic practices of a remote Siberian tribe in 1901, reported that disembodied voices could be heard during the shaman's rituals. Bogoras captured these sounds while recording the drum-beating of the shaman. Not just one, but several voices were heard, speaking in both English (a language known but not familiar to the shaman) and Russian. Similarly, in Voudon (Voodoo) rituals, when a *Mambo* (a Voudon priestess) opens her govi jars to release the spirits of the dead and speak with them, more than one spirit voice can often be heard, even though the Mambo is typically alone in the small, tent-like structure where the ritual is performed.

The basis of physical mediumship is something called *ectoplasm*, the energy that the spirit draws from the medium. The word was coined by Professor Charles Richet in 1894. It comes from the Greek *ekto* and *plasma*, meaning "exteriorized substance." It's actually a white substance that oozes out of the medium's body from various orifices (ears, nostrils, eyes). It can morph into a rigid rod, which can then be used to move items or levitate the table. It can also "clothe" the visiting spirit, thus causing it to resemble the traditional ghost dressed in a white sheet. (That particular image actually comes from the time when the dead were buried in *winding sheets*, shrouds or strips of cloth in which the body was wrapped.) In a darkened séance room—and incidentally, it seems that the presence of bright light prevents the manufacture of ectoplasm, so most séances are conducted in the dark—the white, almost phosphorescent quality of the ectoplasm allows the sitters to actually see the visiting spirit. Many infrared photographs have been taken during such séances, proving that there is no fraud involved.

This was not always the case, however. In the early days of Spiritualism, when charlatans were attracted by the opportunity to make money from vulnerable grieving relatives, fraudulent mediums would swallow lengths of cheesecloth or something similar, and then, under cover of darkness, regurgitate them as though they were ectoplasm. With the advent of infrared photography, these charlatans were quickly exposed, even while the genuine article was endorsed. According to Sir Arthur Conan Doyle in his book *The History of Spiritualism* (1924), the first spirit photographs were taken by Richard Boursnell, an English photographer, in 1851. However, more details subsequently emerged regarding one William H. Mumler of Boston, Massachusetts, who is now generally recognized as the pioneer of the field. In 1861 Mumler, a jewel engraver, was visiting the studio of a friend. While he waited for the friend to finish his work, Mumler amused himself by trying to take a self-portrait. Typical of the times, he focused the camera on a chair, tripped the shutter, removed the cover from the lens, and then ran forward to stand beside the chair and waited for the shutter to open. When he developed the plate he was amazed to find that there was a figure of a young girl in the picture with him. She was sitting on the chair but it was possible to see the chair through her. He recognized her as his cousin who had died 12 years previously. He inscribed the back of the photograph as follows: "This photograph was taken of myself, by myself, on Sunday, when there was not a living soul in the room beside me—so to speak. The form on my right I recognize as my cousin, who passed away about twelve years since."[5]

Just as there were (and still are) fraudulent mediums, so were there fraudulent spirit photographers. Many if not most of the earliest photographs of ghosts were created through double exposure and other simple tricks. Of course, just because it is possible to produce something fraudulently does not mean that all such photographs are fakes. Far from it. There were a number of well-defined pictures that were thoroughly examined and acknowledged by the experts of the day to be genuine. One of these was Mumler's later portrait of Mary Todd Lincoln, the wife of the assassinated president. The appointment for her to be photographed was set up by her friends, using false names for themselves and referring to her as "Mrs. Tyndall." Mumler prepared as he usually did for his sitter, believing her to be a Boston widow. When the plate of her portrait was developed, a figure could be seen standing behind her. A woman present looked at it and exclaimed, "Why, that looks like President Lincoln!" It was only then that "Mrs. Tyndall" said, "Yes it does. I am his widow." Today, with Photoshop and the like, it is relatively easy to fake a photograph of a ghost, but even so, there are many authentic ones still being taken.

How do ghosts make their presence known? The ghost of Charles Rosna did it by tapping on the ceiling and walls. Other ghosts may actually appear as a solid or transparent form. But oftentimes, the indications of the presence of a ghost or spirit are far more subtle. A light may be found on in a room where you were certain you had turned it off; cabinet doors may be found open when you know you had closed them; or the television may turn itself on and off. These and other clues are often left by a spirit who wants to be recognized. In such cases it is invariably a deceased loved one or acquaintance trying to make contact. If this happens to you, accept that you are not alone. If you have suspicions as to who it is, say so out loud. If you have no idea who it might be, say something like, "I don't know who you are, but welcome!" Then try to set up some system of communication—for example, suggest that the spirit blink the lights, or move the cabinet door a certain number of times for yes and a different number for no.

It's not easy for a ghost to affect physical objects, so don't be surprised if you get nothing more than that initial indication of contact. But be aware that other attempts to get your attention may occur in the future. If you cannot sit down and have a séance right away, at least try to give the spirit all of your attention; this could involve simply sitting quietly and meditating. Many times spirits can come through relatively easily during meditation. Another means of spirit contact is through dreams; people often find themselves dreaming of a recently deceased loved one, not realizing that it's not just a figment of that person but actual contact from the person's spirit.

Why do ghosts visit us? There are a number of possible reasons. In the case of Charles Rosna, it was to let people know what had happened to him and, eventually, to bring about the discovery of his body. In similar cases it may be to say a final farewell, or just to have a last look at all that was familiar. Sometimes, as I've already mentioned, it is because of the way the person died. If it was an especially traumatic death, it may be very difficult for the spirit to let go and accept that physical life has truly ended. Some ghosts seem to be drawn back to the scene of their death on its anniversary. With some, it's as though there were a kind of metaphysical DVD that keeps playing over and over again. This can be seen with many historical events when large numbers of people have died. In Gettysburg, Pennsylvania, for example, approximately 8,000 soldiers died during that conflict. Reports of encounters with ghosts in that area are common, many of them on the first through the third of July, the anniversary of the battle in 1863. At Little Big Horn, Montana, reports of ghosts are common, both of members the Seventh Cavalry Regiment and of the Native American Sioux Nation. They are often seen on the anniversary of the June 25, 1876 massacre. Abraham Lincoln's ghost has also been seen on the anniversary of his assassination. In more recent times, Rudolph Valentino, the silent screen actor (and a great believer in spirit communication), has been seen at his former home, Falcon Lair, on August 15, the anniversary of his death. Interestingly enough, although Valentino actually died in a hotel in New York City, his ghost always appears at his former home in Bel Air, which was so important to him.

Sometimes a ghost is not a true ghost in the sense that it is not a manifestation of a deceased person. It is, in effect, a "living ghost"—a manifestation of someone who is astrally projecting.

Some occultists claim that there is a plane that exists between the physical one and the one we go to after death (the Spirit World). That middle level is the astral plane. It is here, they say, where our spirit also goes during sleep, trance, or deep meditation. The physical body has an invisible double known as the *etheric body* or *astral body*; this is thought to be the actual spirit of a person. In sleep, this astral body will sometimes leave the physical body and go on journeys: to visit places fondly remembered, to satisfy curiosity, or just to indulge in a respite from the stresses of everyday life. When an astral body is on such a journey, an especially sensitive psychic will sometimes glimpse that astral double and believe it is a ghost.

One type of ghost that does not really fit the description of a departed spirit is the poltergeist. The word means "noisy ghost," and comes from the German *polte*, meaning "noise," and *geist*, meaning "ghost." A poltergeist is probably no more than a raw psychic energy field. Poltergeist activity is frequently encountered in the presence of a young person, an adolescent going through puberty, or someone in a highly volatile emotional state. That person is invariably unaware of the energy they are giving off until the poltergeist activity literally explodes. When this happens, objects will levitate, fly through the air, and crash into walls or smash on the floor. Lights will flash on and off, and doors will open and slam shut. Ordinary objects will become veritable missiles as they are hurled through the air by this unseen psychic force. This has been incorrectly described as a malevolent energy, but it is not that at all; it is undirected energy with no purpose, neither good nor evil.

Poltergeist activity has been recorded around the world since ancient times. In an analysis of 500 such cases since 1800, researchers A. D. Cornell and Alan Gauld found that 12 percent of the cases involved the repeated opening and closing of doors and windows, 24 percent lasted more than a year, 36 percent involved moving large pieces of furniture, 48 percent included rapping sounds, 58 percent were most active at night, and 64 percent involved the moving of small objects. In the 1960s, William G. Roll, of the Psychical Research Foundation in Durham, North Carolina, studied 116 cases going back four centuries and concluded that when a particular person was present during the phenomena, the activity was due to expressions of unconscious psychokinesis. *Psychokinesis*, or PK, is the movement of objects without physical contact, by the power of the mind alone.

Ghosts, then, are a nearly universal phenomenon. They can be seen or heard—or both. They can frighten or they can assuage grief. But if we accept them for what they are, as manifestations of spirits of the deceased, we can communicate with them and possibly learn more about the life that exists beyond that transition we call death. Andrew Jackson Davis said that "the term spirit is used to signify the centermost principle of man's existence; the divine energy or life of the soul of Nature."[6] Nandor Fodor described it as "the inmost principle, the divine particle, the vital essence, the inherent actuating element in life."[7] As such, "spirit" implies immortal life. If that is the case, it stands to reason that ghosts are here to stay. Whether we decide to talk to them or not is another matter entirely.

Notes

1. Quoted by Barbara Weisberg in *Talking to the Dead: Kate and Maggie Fox and the Rise of Spiritualism* (San Francisco: Harper, 2004), 23.

2. Ibid, 24.

3. The Foxes were Methodists. "Mr. Splitfoot" was a term for the Devil, who was thought to have cloven hooves.

4. Conan-Doyle, Arthur, *The History of Spiritualism, Vol. 1* (London: Doran, 1924), 69.

5. Mumler, William, *Personal Experiences of William H. Mumler in Spirit Photography* (Boston, 1875).

6. Davis, Andrew Jackson, *Principles of Nature* (New York: S. S. Lyon and W. Fishbough, 1847).

7. Fodor, Nandor, *Encyclopedia of Psychic Science* (London: Arthur's Press, 1934).

Are Spirits All Around Us?

By Michael E. Tymn

Millions of spiritual creatures walk the earth
Unseen, both when we wake and when we sleep.

—Milton

To understand the complexities of an imperceptible spirit world and how the activities within that world influence us, one must first set aside the dichotomous humdrum heaven and horrific hell of orthodox religion and instead consider a more multifaceted afterlife—one in which there are perhaps as many degrees of good and evil as we find in our material world.

Although orthodoxy has as its foundation a belief in an afterlife, there is much disagreement among various religions as to the nature of that afterlife, including the activity and location of any spirits therein. If we define spirits as discarnate or deceased humans, orthodoxy believes that they are all in a deep sleep until a day of judgment—or they are slumbering in some staging area awaiting entrance to heaven—or they are purging their sins in purgatory—or they are already in heaven, where they must be strumming harps while endlessly praising God 24/7. Of course, they may also be in hell, or awaiting condemnation to that place of everlasting torment and punishment. Again, the specific beliefs vary according to religion and denomination, but the after-life itself is still a necessary component to all of them.

If we tread outside of the self-imposed limits of mainstream religious dogma, however, we find that the spirits of the dead, rather than being relegated to some other plane, are actually all around us. Some are advanced and guiding us in positive ways (while being careful not to impose on our free will), whereas some are "earthbound" and influencing us in negative ways. In between these guiding and misguiding spirits, we can find many wandering around in a stupor of sorts, still awakening in the spirit world while clinging to their old earthly homes and friends, and still others who are fully awakened and are content to just check in on us now and then while partaking of the many activities available to them in this new plane of existence. In the Bible, John 14:2 reads, "In my Father's house are many mansions. If it were not so, I would have told you." The Greek word for "mansions" might have been translated more accurately as "abodes." Religious leaders have long struggled with interpreting this passage, the most accepted interpretation of which is that some spirits reside closer to God than others, even though they are all in heaven. However, modern revelation—which comes to us through credible mediumship, out-of-body travel, near-death experiences, past-life regressions, and various forms of mysticism—suggests that the afterlife is made up of many planes, realms, spheres, dimensions, states, or abodes. A number of spirit messengers communicating through mediums have reported that there are seven basic planes in the afterlife, thus giving some credence to "seventh heaven" mythology. According to these messengers, the seventh plane is where we experience perfect bliss and oneness with God—what the Buddhists call *Nirvana*. These same spirit messengers stress, however, that contrary to Buddhist teachings, we do not lose our individuality in this oneness, which might also be called "true heaven"; rather, we attain even greater consciousness and, concomitantly, greater individuality.

The plane nearest to the material world is where we find spiritually—and morally—challenged spirits or souls, those who failed to take advantage of the many opportunities afforded them to expand their consciousness while they were alive. As the afterlife is reportedly a world of consciousness only, many Spiritualists have interpreted the hellfire of orthodox religion as a "fire of the mind" on the lowest plane. In between are planes of progression or advancement. Catholics tend to lump all of these planes together into one place, purgatory. Although the Catholic Church teaches that purgatory is basically a temporary version of hell, the spirit messengers tell us that the planes of progression become more and more pleasant as we advance higher up the "rungs" of the afterlife ladder. The lower planes are usually conceived of as the darker ones, and the higher planes, as the lighter ones. Spiritualists infer from the mediumistic messages that the average decent person who is not particularly spiritually evolved will usually find him- or herself on the third plane, which the Spiritualists call Summerland. Conditions on this plane are reportedly much the same as they are here on the earthly plane.

Afterlife Explorations

Emanuel Swedenborg, an 18th-century Swedish scientist turned mystic, may have been the first person to significantly change the public's attitude toward the idea of an afterlife. Swedenborg abandoned his scientific career at age 56, in 1744, and spent the next 30 years of his life pursuing spiritual truths through clairvoyant trances and out-of-body travel. He wrote extensively on his forays into the afterlife environment, stating that there is much diversity and "countless communities" in the hereafter.[1] He further reported that the world of spirits is neither heaven nor hell, but rather a place or state between the two, and that angels are in heaven while spirits are in the spirit world. Edgar Cayce, the famous American "sleeping prophet" of the early decades of the last century, also told of taking a tour of many realms during one of his out-of-body experiences. He described how he encountered a stream of light he knew he must follow. In the lower or darker realms he saw souls who were floundering or lost and seeking the light. As the light grew stronger and stronger, he arrived at a place where the spirits or souls resembled living people.

Communicating with his daughter through the British clairvoyant Margaret Flavell Tweedell, Alvin Mattson, who had been a Lutheran minister in his earthly life, declared that "all of the various planes of consciousness have different frequencies of vibration."[2] Mattson said that he was in the astral world, and that souls could progress from there to the higher planes. "By 'higher' planes," he added, "I do not mean spatially higher, but rather those planes which have a finer vibration."[3] Mattson also said that the astral world is almost an exact replica of our world, except that it is of a finer substance and its inhabitants are not bound to objective reality, as we are.

In 1853, Dr. Robert Hare, an emeritus professor of chemistry at the University of Pennsylvania, began investigating mediums and assumed that he would expose them all as frauds. However, he came to recognize that some were genuine; he even developed mediumistic abilities of his own. While sitting with Margaret Gourlay, a gifted medium, Hare heard from a spirit named Maria, the deceased daughter of a personal friend. Maria said that she was living on the fourth plane, which she called "an enchanted land,"[4] but her brother William greeted her when she regained consciousness on that side and gave her a tour of the second and third planes. On the second plane, she found "moral darkness pervading the atmosphere, rendering it gloomy and uncomfortable in the extreme."[5] She said that the inhabitants there appeared dark and dismal and seemed to be continually tortured with the pangs of a guilty conscience. There was much disorder and confusion. This plane is very much reminiscent of the Catholic purgatory. "Its denizens are seen straggling here and there, with no fixed object in view," Maria related. "All are seeking to minister to their perverted tastes. Some are holding forth in loud tones, and painting in false and gaudy colors the joy of their home; others, who occupied high stations on earth, hang their heads in confusion, and would fain hide themselves from view."[6] In contrast, Maria observed order and beauty on the third plane. She said that the scenery there was endlessly diverse and corresponded to that of the earthly plane.

Nearly all psychic travelers or spirit communicators report a progression from darkness to light, from unconsciousness to consciousness, from spiritual depravity to spiritual enlightenment, from ignorance to knowledge, and from imperfection to perfection. They also report that the rate of vibration of the individual spirit or soul increases with this progression; thus, those on the higher planes vibrate at a much higher rate than those on the lower planes. They further state that the higher the vibration, the more difficult it is to communicate with those still in the earthly plane. Thus, advanced spirits may find it necessary to relay messages through spirits on lower realms, in which case the messages are sometimes distorted by devious low-level spirits. Such spirits are able to get through much more easily, and often represent themselves as enlightened spirits in attempts to mislead those still in the material world. Although orthodox religion generally frowns on all forms of spirit communication, the New Testament passage 1 John 4:1 advises that we should "test the spirits whether they are of God," while 1 Corinthians 12:10 talks about "discernment" of spiritual messages. Orthodox leaders fail to explain why we should bother to "test" and "discern" such messages if spirit communication is prohibited in the first place, or if, as we are told in Deuteronomy 18:10–12 in the Old Testament, the "dead know nothing."

Moral Specific Gravity

One's initial place in this multi-layered afterlife is apparently the result of what was referred to by Professor Hare as *moral specific gravity*. In his many conversations with spirit communicators, Hare was informed that a person's good works (or lack thereof) manifest in his or her energy field, often referred to as the *aura*. Thus, after death, a soul will gravitate to either darkness or light, according to how moral the person was here on Earth. Hare was also informed by actual spirits that people cannot "cheat" and skip to higher realms, as each person's moral specific gravity will allow him or her to tolerate only so much light. If a spirit were to try to enter a realm that he or she is not ready or qualified for, he or she would not be able to endure the searing brightness.

Like Swedenborg, Frederick C. Schulthorp, an Englishman, learned how to explore the afterlife via out-of-body travel and clairvoyance. He was told by spirit entities that every thought generates an electrical impulse, which is then imprinted upon the person's energy field and stored there. The sum total of all the vibrations throughout the person's lifetime determines his or her initial station in the afterlife. "Upon entry into spirit life, a person will naturally and automatically gravitate to his state in spirit which corresponds to his acts and thoughts throughout life as reproduced by his 'personal tape record.'"[7] Indeed, more than a century previous to Schulthorp's discoveries, the Reverend Arthur Chambers, an associate of King's College, London, and Vicar of the Church of England in Brockenhurst, Hampshire, claimed that a spirit talking through a medium told him this, as well: "Persons enter the Spiritual World with precisely the same character, enlightenment and disposition as that with which they leave your world and go into a sphere for which they are fitted. And there they remain until mentally, morally, and spiritually advanced, they are fitted for a higher sphere."[8]

Earthbound Spirits

People who communicate with sprits often report that many souls remain in an earthbound condition after they die, meaning that they did not "go into the light." This is most often a result of having lived a materialistic or depraved lifestyle. Or, to put it another way, these souls did not develop a significant spiritual consciousness while in the flesh. Many of these earthbound spirits do not even realize they are dead. According to Swedenborg, the spiritually oriented person is quick to recognize his or her transition, but the sense-bound person may take years or even centuries to recognize that he or she has passed on. Allan Kardec, the pioneering French psychical investigator of the 19th century, explained it this way:

> The duration of the state of confusion that follows death varies greatly. It may be only a few hours, and it may be several months, or even years. Those with whom it lasts the least are they who, during the earthly life, have identified themselves most closely with their future state, because they are soonest able to understand their new situation.[9]

Edgar Cayce said that "many an individual has remained in that called death for what ye call years without realizing it was dead!"[10] Cayce further explained that the "entity" becomes conscious gradually and that this is contingent upon "how great are the appetites and desires of a physical body."[11] A very similar message comes from the extensive writings of the medium Alice Bailey and her teacher, the Tibetan master Djwhal Khul:

> In the case of the [spiritually] undeveloped person, the etheric body can linger for a long time in the neighborhood of its outer disintegrating shell because the pull of the soul is not potent and the material aspect is. Where the person is advanced, and therefore detached in his thinking from the physical plane, the dissolution of the vital body can be exceedingly rapid.[12]

It is difficult to understand how someone could not know whether he or she is dead. But if you ask yourself whether you know you are alive when you are dreaming, it becomes a bit easier to grasp. In effect, the earthbound spirit is experiencing something akin to a bad dream or nightmare, perhaps that "fire of the mind" referred to by Spiritualists. As these earthbound spirits progress from the lower to the higher planes, they slowly become more and more aware of their condition. Even when they recognize that they are dead, however, they may remain bewildered and confused, in a kind of stupor or semi-consciousness. According to the spirits communicating with Hare, the number of spirits on the first two planes far outnumbers those on the five planes above them.

Earthbound spirits, whether they are aware of their physical death or not, tend to flounder in the vibrational vicinity of the earth plane. "Not knowing where to go or what to do, most such souls start to wander, either aimlessly or else to some chosen place or person," explains Dr. Louise Ireland-Frey in *Freeing Captives*. "We call these souls wanderers."[13] Many of these wanderers, she adds, move into what turns out to be the body or aura of a living person and become attached entities, often without the living person *or* the invading spirit even being aware of the relationship. There are, according to Ireland-Frey, several degrees of attachment, beginning with temptation, followed by influencing or shadowing, then oppression, obsession, and finally, possession. In the first two, the hovering entity will affect the living person only mildly, with symptoms ranging from temptations and mood swings to irrationality and sudden inexplicable fear or depression. In oppression, the entity is affecting the living person's behavior more noticeably and frequently. In obsession, the entity may actually invade the individual's psyche and meld its own personality traits with those of the host, resulting in much confusion and bewilderment. And with possession, the entity takes over the body of the living person completely, pushing out the host's personality and resulting in bizarre changes in behavior.

Ireland-Frey was no sawbones physician. She graduated *Phi Beta Kappa* from Colorado University, then earned a master's degree from Mount Holyoke College and an MD from Tulane University. It was not until late in her medical career, while studying hypnotherapy, that she came to understand and deal with the ills caused by spirit attachment. As Ireland-Frey and others who have recognized the attachment phenomenon have pointed out, like attracts like, and so a deceased alcoholic may look for a living alcoholic to "feed" off of, while a former sex addict will likely look for someone with similar proclivities. Although mainstream psychiatry and psychology scoff at the idea that mental problems could be the result of spirit influence, more and more credible practitioners have publicly announced their belief in such a phenomenon and have focused their practice on something called *spirit release therapy.*

Spirit Release Therapy

According to Dr. Stafford Betty, professor of religious studies at California State University at Bakersfield,

> a new breed of therapist is healing the mentally ill not with talk and drug therapy, but by releasing troublesome or malevolent spirits who have attached themselves to their victims. I am not talking about religious healers like Francis McNutt, but secular healers, some of them licensed psychiatrists or psychologists, who have discovered, often by accident, that this new therapy works better than what they learned in medical or graduate school. They tell us that too often drug therapy only masks symptoms, and talk therapy reaches only as deep as the patient's conscious mind can go. But "spirit release" usually heals, often permanently. Not only does it heal the client; it heals the attached (or "possessing") spirit.[14]

Although Kardec had already recognized the possession phenomenon during the 1850s, Dr. Carl Wickland, an American psychiatrist, became the real pioneer of spirit "depossession" during the early part of the last century. In his 1924 book, *Thirty Years Among the Dead*, Wickland described how he drove spirits from a patient's body into that of his wife, Anna, a medium, by means of static electricity. While these earthbound spirits were occupying Anna's body, Wickland was able to communicate with them and persuade them to leave. Wickland claimed to have dislodged 13 different spirits; in one case alone, seven spirits were recognized by the patient's mother as relatives or friends who had since passed. One had been the minister of their Methodist church. He had been killed in a train accident nine years earlier but was still unaware that he had died. Another of Wickland's patients was a pharmacist who had become addicted to drugs, particularly morphine. After the static electricity treatment was administered to the patient, the obsessing spirit jumped into Anna's entranced body and began coughing violently. Wickland asked what the problem was, and the spirit replied that she was dying and needed some morphine. Wickland explained to her that she was already dead, but the spirit ignored his comments and continued to beg for morphine. Wickland managed to calm the spirit down enough to further explain the situation to her and ask her for a name. At first she couldn't remember, but after several moments of searching gave her name as Elizabeth Noble. She said that she was 42 years old and was living in El Paso, Texas. After begging for morphine once again, she noticed her deceased husband, Frank, standing there next to her in spirit. Frank Noble then took over Anna's body and explained to Wickland that he had died before his wife and had been trying to get her to realize she had "passed out," but so far had been unsuccessful. He thanked Wickland for explaining the situation to her and said that she would now understand and be able to heal and move on.

On April 4, 1923, a "Mrs. V." came to Wickland for treatment of her alcoholism. As soon as the obsessing spirit (a male) took hold of Anna, he commented that he was just about to have a drink and have a good time when he was interrupted by Wickland. He complained of someone "pouring fire" all over him (ostensibly, the static electricity).[15] He identified himself as Paul Hopkins, and spoke of "Mrs. V." as his friend who frequently gave him "good whiskey" to drink. After a lengthy conversation, Wickland was able to convince Hopkins that he was dead. Once he accepted that fact, he saw his mother there in spirit to help him adjust and move on. Wickland recorded that "Mrs. V." had no further desire for alcohol after their session.

Despite these amazing documented cases, mainstream psychiatry wanted nothing to do with such superstitious beliefs, which supposedly had been put behind us several centuries ago. Slowly and gradually, however, professionals are starting to see the light and have the courage to incorporate spirit release therapy into their practices. In 1999, the Spirit Release Foundation (SRF) was formed, and its membership now numbers around 150. The SRF Website lists eight common "side effects" of spirit attachment:

1. Unexplained fatigue.
2. Unexplained depression.
3. Sudden changes in mood.
4. Hearing voices.
5. Addictions of all sorts.
6. Uncharacteristic changes in personality or behavior.
7. Anomalous sexual behavior.
8. Unexplained somatic symptoms.

The foundation is careful to note, however, that there are often other, more prosaic causes for such symptoms.

The spirit release therapy of today is analogous to exorcism. It usually involves direct communication between the attached spirit and the therapist. The patient is usually put into a trance by hypnosis or by following an image or feeling. "Having established contact with the earthbound spirit, it is necessary to persuade it to leave," Dr. Alan Sanderson, president of the SRF, explains. "Should there be any reluctance on the part of the patient, host and entity are told that both are being harmed by the attachment, and the matter must be resolved."[16] (If the earthbound spirit is unwilling to leave, the therapist may call for a loved one or spirit guide from the light to assist in persuading the entity to leave. "They see the procedure not as a throwback to medieval times, when demoniacs were put to death, but as an advance,"

Professor Betty says of the therapy, adding that "Dr. William Woolger, an internationally renowned transpersonal psychologist, sees it as the next and essential stage in the development of psychology, a kind of return to the source."[17]

Tortured, Tormented, and Troubled Souls

Tortured, tormented, or troubled souls often remain in an earthbound condition, apparently aware of the fact that they have left the material world but unable to go into the light until some earthly matter is resolved. For example, in her 2006 book *A Voice from the Grave*, Christine Holohan, an Irish medium living in England, tells of being contacted by the spirit of a young woman named Jacqui Poole, who had been murdered several days earlier. The woman provided details of the murder and the name of her killer, all of which were passed on to the police. However, while the initially skeptical police became convinced that the man named by the murdered woman was, in fact, the guilty person, they were not able to arrest him until DNA testing became available some 18 years later, at which time the man was convicted and sentenced to life in prison. During those 18 years, Jacqui continually came to Christine, pleading for her to do something that was just not in her power to do. It wasn't until after the murderer was brought to justice that Jacqui left Christine and apparently went into the light.

Spirit messengers have reported that the grief of loved ones left behind weighs heavily on departed souls and keeps them earthbound, as well. "We don't know that through our great sorrow and despair we tie our beloved soul with great virtual chains thereby doing a great wrong—without mentioning the wrong we do ourselves," states Wanda Pratnicka, a Polish psychotherapist. "Grief and despair will not allow [the departed soul] to leave even though it has the right and energy to do so, and at the appropriate time, too."[18]

Such was the message communicated by Olive Thomas, a popular Hollywood actress of the silent-screen era, who died of a drug overdose in September of 1920. Communicating with J. Gay Stevens, a New York journalist and a member of the American Society for Psychical Research, through the medium Chester Michael Grady, Thomas informed Stevens that she needed to get word to her mother that her death was accidental, not a scandalous suicide as had been reported by the press. The mother was apparently in despair over the thought that her daughter had taken her own life. Thomas explained to Stevens that when she couldn't sleep she reached for a bottle of sleeping pills but took the wrong bottle, one very similar in appearance. It contained bichloride of mercury, which killed her. When Stevens contacted Thomas's mother, the mother wanted nothing to do with him, assuming that, as a journalist, he was just trying to add to the scandal. Moreover, her pastor told her that he was probably an agent of the devil.

Thomas insisted, however, that Stevens keep trying. She then provided some evidentiary support that she felt certain would convince her mother that she was alive in the spirit world and communicating. She said that all of her jewelry had been returned to her mother after her death except one item, her favorite brooch. She told Stevens that the brooch got caught up in the lining of a pocket in the steamer trunk now in her mother's attic. She also told Stevens one of the pearls, the third from the top on the right, had come out of its setting and was loose in the tissue paper surrounding the brooch. When Stevens brought this information to Thomas's mother, she reluctantly agreed to go to the attic and search the steamer trunk. Finding the brooch with the loose pearl was enough to convince her that it was her daughter, and not Satan, who was communicating with her. She accepted the explanation that her daughter did not commit suicide, and this clearly relieved much of her grief and released the daughter to move on.

Strong regrets may also prevent a soul from going into the light. In a sitting with Boston medium Leonora Piper, the Rev. W.H. Savage was told that someone named Robert West was there and wanted Savage to give his brother, Minot, a message. West said he wanted to apologize for something he had written "in advance."[19] Savage did not understand the message but passed it on to Minot, who understood it and explained that West had been the editor of a publication called the *Advance* and had criticized Minot's work in an editorial. When Dr. Minot Savage sat with Mrs. Piper, he heard from his deceased son, who had died at age 31 three years earlier. "Papa, I want you to go at once to my room," Savage recalled his son communicating with a great deal of earnestness. "Look in my drawer and you will find a lot of loose papers. Among them are some which I would like you to take and destroy at once."[20] The son had lived with a friend in Boston and his personal effects had remained there after his death. Savage went to his son's room and searched the drawer, gathering up all the loose papers. "There were things there which he had jotted down and trusted to the privacy of his drawer which he would not have made public for the world," Savage related, commenting that he would not violate his son's privacy by disclosing the contents of the papers.[21]

Unfinished or lost wills have also anchored souls to the earthly realm. One of the victims of the 1915 sinking of the *Lusitania* by a German U-boat was Sir Hugh Lane, an art connoisseur and director of the National Gallery of Ireland in Dublin. He was transporting lead boxes containing paintings of Monet, Rembrandt, Rubens, and Titian, which were insured for $4 million and were to be displayed at the National Gallery. Hester Travers Smith, an Irish medium, and Lennox Robinson, a renowned Irish playwright, were sitting at a Ouija board one night when Lane began communicating with them. "I am Hugh Lane, all is dark," the planchette spelled out, although Travers Smith and Robinson were blindfolded and so had no clue as to what the message was.[22] In fact, they were conversing on other matters as their hands moved rapidly. After several minutes, the Rev. Savell Hicks, who was jotting down the messages, told Travers Smith and Robinson that it was Sir Hugh Lane coming through and that he told them he had been aboard the *Lusitania* and had drowned.

Although they had heard of the disaster, none of the three was aware that Lane had been a passenger on the ship. They continued receiving messages from Lane, again, providing evidentiary support for the spirit's claims. His main concern seemed to be that a codicil to his will be honored. He had left his private collection of art to the National Gallery in London, but the codicil stated that they should go to the National Gallery in Dublin. Because he had not signed the codicil, the London gallery was reluctant to give them up. "Those pictures must be secured for Dublin," Lane communicated on January 22, 1918, going on to say that he could not rest until they were.[23] Unfortunately, I was never able to discover the outcome of this story. I sent an e-mail to the National Gallery in Dublin a few years ago and they did not respond, so for all we know, Lane's spirit may still be unquiet.

There are many other stories suggesting that we take our concerns, anxieties, mistakes, and regrets with us to the afterlife, but the biggest regret of all seems to come from not finding out more about the spirit world when we were alive. Communicating with Allan Kardec, the distinguished French researcher of the 19th century, a spirit identified as Van Durst, who had been employed by the government before dying at age 88 in 1863, told Kardec that he very much regretted not paying any attention to spiritual matters before his death. "If, before quitting the earth, I had known what you know, how much more easy and agreeable would have been my initiation into this other life," Van Durst's spirit said. "I should have known, before dying, what I had to learn afterwards, at the moment of separation; and my soul would have accomplished its disengagement much more easily."[24]

Positive Influences

As we have already learned, investigators and explorers of the spirit world tell us that spirits from the middle and higher planes are often around us, too, but that their influence is much more subtle, as they are more respectful of our individuality and free will than are the spirits occupying the lower planes. "Spirits of the higher spheres control more or less those below them in station, who are sent by them to impress mortals virtuously," Professor Hare explained, referring to what he had come to understand from various spirits. "Spirits are not allowed to interpose directly, so as to alter the course of events upon earth. They are not allowed to aid in any measure to obtain wealth."[25] Hare's deceased brother informed him that his mission was to instruct spirits in the lower planes and to help raise them from their degraded condition, but went on to say that every spirit has a sphere of utility and that many of them are involved in assisting those still in on the earth plane. However, he was quick to point out that spirits are limited in what they can do and impart: "[L]et them be undeceived, for it is utterly impossible for them to comprehend all in their present rudimental state," he stated, referring to those still in the flesh.[26]

During the middle decades of the last century, a spirit named Silver Birch, believed to be an advanced group soul, communicated through the British trance medium Maurice Barbanell. It said that there are spirits all around us who take an interest in our activities. "Though they do not speak to you, and you cannot hear them, they are here, each striving to do the utmost to assist you," Silver Birch explained. "They are closer than you know. They know your secrets, the unspoken desires of your minds, your wishes, your hopes, and your fears."[27] Silver Birch went on to say that they attempt to guide us so that we can extract the lessons necessary for soul growth.

Swedenborg and other spirit-world explorers have reported that these spirit guides are similar to their charges in terms of sensibility, intelligence, spirituality, and so on, and that therefore they are often changed several times during a person's lifetime in order to keep pace with his or her development and growth. Thus, a spiritually advanced person will have more advanced spirits guiding him or her, as there must be a certain harmony of mind between them. Conversely, someone still in the elementary stages of spiritual evolution would not benefit from an advanced spirit guide, as there would be too much of a disconnect between them. (Otherwise it would be like trying to take a course in advanced algebra without first taking elementary and intermediate algebra.) According to Imperator, believed to be an advanced spirit, as it communicated through the Rev. William Stainton Moses, an Anglican minister, there is a certain magnetic rapport that exists between a person and his or her guide. However, the rapport can only take place if the person allows his or her inner nature to be open to it. "[I]t is those of you who live most in the spirit who penetrate deepest into the hidden mysteries," Imperator explained. "We can come nearest to them. We can touch hidden cords in their nature which vibrate only to our touch, and are never stirred by your world's influences. 'Tis they who reach highest in their earth-life, for they have learned already to commune with spirit, and are fed with spiritual food."[28]

Andrew Jackson Davis, known as the "Poughkeepsie Seer" because of his special clairvoyance and ability to explore the spirit world, addressed the question as to why spirit guides (or guardian angels, as they are sometimes called) don't always protect us from harm. He explained that this is because one's inner being is not open to spirit influence. He further said that we must all undergo adversity in order to properly experience life and evolve spiritually. The spirits told Allan Kardec much the same thing. "They willingly enter into communication with those who seek truth in simplicity and sincerity and who are sufficiently freed from the bonds of materiality to be capable of understanding it," he related. "But they turn from those whose inquiries are prompted only by curiosity, or who are drawn away from the path of rectitude by the attractions of materiality."[29] In effect, our guides can assist us only when we are open to and in rapport with them. Or, to put it another way, the more materialistic the person is, the less likely it is that he or she will be in tune with and/or influenced by his/her guide.

Child prodigies

It may be that child prodigies are a result of spirit influence, although it is not clear whether this is the influence of earthbound spirits who were gifted during their earthly lives and are now frustrated, or of more advanced spirits who simply want to enrich our lives. Communicating spirits told Kardec that spirits are inclined to influence those for whom they have a certain affection, so it seems that the latter is more likely to be true. Dr. Charles Richet, the 1913 Nobel Prize winner in medicine, reported on the strange case of Pepito Arriola, who, at age 3 years and 3 months, performed at the Psychological Congress in Paris in the year 1900. Richet stated that the boy played the piano brilliantly: "He composed military or funeral marches, waltzes, habaneras, minuets, and played some twenty difficult pieces from memory," Richet wrote. "A hundred members of the Congress heard and applauded him."[30] It was further reported that little

Pepito's hands could not stretch more than five notes, yet he appeared to be able to play full octaves (eight notes). Some onlookers said that his hands seemed to increase in size during the playing, and Rosalie Thompson, a clairvoyant, claimed that she saw the child dissolve into the figure of a man while he was at the piano. Pepito's mother, herself an accomplished musician, stated that she never taught her son to play. Her first awareness of the boy's talent was when he was just 2 and half years old. She heard one of her own difficult pieces being played flawlessly, entered the room, and found her son at the piano.

Genetics may be a factor in the sense that the spirits seem to seek out people who already have the innate talent for whatever ability it is they are trying to impart. Spirit operators explained to medium William Stainton Moses that because he had no real musical appreciation, they could not produce proper music through him. Communicating through direct-voice medium Leslie Flint in 1956, the spirit of the composer Chopin mentioned that during his time here on earth, he had been aware of "beings" giving him inspiration and assistance while he was composing. In fact, he cited this as his sole reason for making such an effort to contact the living. He was grateful for having had this otherworldly help, and he wanted to extend this same help to others.

Spirits are indeed all around us. Their influence ranges from the very negative to the very positive, depending on the state of the spirit and the receptivity of the person involved. Someone with a highly evolved spiritual consciousness will have a strong energy field, or aura, and therefore repel the negative and absorb the positive, while someone with very little spiritual consciousness and a correspondingly weak aura will attract the negative and repel the positive. As the majority of people are somewhere in the middle, the forces of light are continually doing battle with the forces of darkness on the inner planes. In these times of terror, chaos, strife, and uncertainty, by all appearances the forces of darkness are winning the war. What will happen in the end remains to be seen.

Notes

1. Swedenborg, Emanuel, *Heaven and Hell* (West Chester, Pa.: The Swedenborg Foundation, 1976), 40.

2. Taylor, Ruth Mattson, *Witness From Beyond* (New York: Hawthorn Books, Inc., 1975), 41.

3. Ibid.

4. Hare, Robert, *Experimental Investigation of the Spirit Manifestation* (New York: Partridge & Brittan, 1855), 105.

5. Ibid.

6. Ibid.

7. Schulthorp, Frederick C, *Excursion to the Spirit World* (London: The Greater World Assoc., 1961), 106.

8. Chambers, Arthur, *Man and the Spiritual World* (Philadelphia: George W. Jacobs & Co., 1900), 167.

9. Kardec, Allan, *The Spirits' Book* (Apartado, Mexico: Amapse Society Mexico, 1857), 118.

10. Cayce, Edgar and Hugh Lynn, *No Death: God's Other Door* (Virginia Beach, Va.: A.R.E. Press, 1998), 48.

11. Ibid.

12. Bailey, Alice A., *Death: The Great Adventure* (New York: Lucis Publishing Co., 1985), 69.

13. Ireland-Frey, Louise, *Freeing Captives.* (Charlottesvile, Va.: Hampton Roads Publishing Co., 1999), 32.

14. Betty, Stafford, "The Searchlight," *Academy of Spirituality and Paranormal Studies* (December 2010): 5.

15. Wickland, Carl A., *Thirty Years Among the Dead* (Van Nuys, Calif.: Newcastle Publishing Co., Inc., 1974 [original publication in 1924]), 171.

16. Sanderson, Alan Lindsay, "Spirit Attachment and Human Health," The Spirit Release Foundation *http://www.spiritrelease.com/review_spiritrelease.htm*. Accessed April 2011.

17. Betty, Stafford, "The Searchlight," *Academy of Spirituality and Paranormal Studies* (December 2010): 5.

18. Pratnicka, Wanda, *Possessed by Ghosts* (Gdynia, Poland: Centrum Publishers, 2006), 82.

19. Holt, Henry, *On the Cosmic Relations* (Boston: Houghton Mifflin Co., 1914), 415.

20. Ibid.

21. Ibid.

22. Travers Smith, Hester, *Voices From the Void* (New York: E. P. Dutton & Company, 1919), 46.

23. Ibid.

24. Kardec, Allan, *Heaven and Hell* (London: Trubner & Co., 1878), 218.

25. Hare, Robert, *Experimental Investigation of the Spirit Manifestation* (New York: Partridge & Brittan, 1855), 124–125.

26. Ibid., 110.

27. Naylor, William, *Silver Birch Anthology* (London: Ebenezer Baylis and Son Ltd., 1955), 60–61.

28. Moses, William Stainton, *Spirit Teachings* (New York: Arno Press, 1976), 104.

29. Kardec, Allan, *The Spirits' Book* (Apartado, Mexico: Amapse Society Mexico, 1857), 100.

30. Richet, Charles, *Thirty Years of Psychical Research* (London: W. Collins & Sons Ltd., 1923), 10.

Bibliography

Bailey, Alice A. *Death: The Great Adventure.* New York: Lucis Publishing Co., 1985.

Betty, Stafford. "The Searchlight." *Academy of Spirituality and Paranormal Studies.* (December 2010).

Cayce, Edgar and Hugh Lynn. *No Death: God's Other Door.* Virginia Beach, Va.: A.R.E. Press, 1998.

Chambers, Arthur. *Man and the Spiritual World.* Philadelphia: George W. Jacobs & Co., 1900.

Davis, Andrew Jackson. *Death and The After-Life.* Boston: Colby & Rich, 1865.

Hare, Robert. *Experimental Investigation of the Spirit Manifestation.* New York: Partridge & Brittan, 1855.

Holohan, Christine. *A Whisper From an Angel.* Meath, Ireland: Maverick House, 2009.

Holt, Henry. *On the Cosmic Relations.* Boston: Houghton Mifflin Co., 1914.

Ireland-Frey, Louise. *Freeing Captives.* Charlottesvile, VA: Hampton Roads Publishing Co., 1999.

Kardec, Allan. *Heaven and Hell.* London: Trubner & Co., 1878.

———. *The Spirits' Book.* Apartado, Mexico: Amapse Society Mexico, 1857.

Moses, William Stainton. *Spirit Teachings.* New York: Arno Press, 1976.

Naylor, William. *Silver Birch Anthology.* London: Ebenezer Baylis and Son Ltd., 1955.

Pratnicka, Wanda. *Possessed by Ghosts.* Gdynia, Poland: Centrum Publishers, 2006.

Richet, Charles. *Thirty Years of Psychical Research.* London: W. Collins & Sons Ltd., 1923

Sanderson, Alan Lindsay. "Spirit Attachment and Human Health." The Spirit Release Foundation. *http://www.spiritrelease.com/ review_spiritrelease.htm.* Accessed April 2011.

Savage, Minot J. *Can Telepathy Explain?* New York: G. P. Putnam's Sons, 1902.

Sculthorp, Frederick C. *Excursion to the Spirit World.* London: The Greater World Assoc., 1961.

Stevens, J. Gay. "The Girl with the Golden Hair." *FATE Magazine.* Dec. 1972, Jan. 1973.

Swedenborg, Emanuel. *Heaven and Hell.* West Chester, PA: The Swedenborg Foundation, 1976.

Taylor, Ruth Mattson. *Witness From Beyond.* New York: Hawthorn Books, Inc., 1975.

Travers Smith, Hester. *Voices From the Void.* New York: E. P. Dutton & Company, 1919.

Wickland, Carl A. *The Gateway of Understanding.* Los Angeles: National Psychological Institute, Inc., 1934.

———. *Thirty Years Among the Dead.* Van Nuys, Calif.: Newcastle Publishing Co., Inc., 1974 (original publication in 1924).

Psychic Gift or Psychotic Nightmare? The Biology of the Supernatural

By Micah A. Hanks

During the course of every person's life, there comes a time when they begin to contemplate their own mortality, and curse the brevity that haunts humanity's singular existence. After all, every person can be certain they will meet their ultimate demise under one circumstance or another. It is only in embracing the underlying unity of humanity as a species that we begin to learn that immortality can indeed be obtained, through the knowledge passed down from those who came before us, and eventually, by passing along our own additions to this cosmic bundle of wisdom to our progeny. It seems only fitting, then, that those who came before us might occasionally appear in our midst, circumventing time, space, and even the inexorable confines of death to impart otherworldly knowledge to us from realms beyond.

Yet how can it be that, for all the wonders afforded us in the world today by the great quasi-religious institution that has become modern science, there is still so much that eludes us? Few would dispute that claims of contact with spirits are indeed improbable and even shocking; therefore, when confronted with such shadows of the immaterial realm, our scientific institutions tend to revert to a willful blindness, dismissing that which cannot be crammed into the mold of human understanding, as a sort of metaphysical nihilism. It is disheartening that the scientific community's attitude toward ghostly visitations is often so negative, especially when we consider how much we still don't know about the human body. Despite all of this rational skepticism regarding the paranormal, many startling cases have been documented that demonstrate at least a correlative link between various strange phenomena and the workings of the human mind and body. Thus, ought we to consider the possibility that there are biological agents within us that might sometimes act as conduits for strange phenomena? Admittedly, this is a bold proposition.

This peculiar idea of biological agents affecting or even governing our experience of the supernatural first came to my attention through a strange set of circumstances shared in a letter from one of the readers of my blog, The Gralien Report. The events related to me had taken place at a small psychiatric center in Port Elizabeth, South Africa, which had been founded to provide in-patient nursing, psychological services, and occupational therapy to approximately 70 residents. Many of these patients are afflicted with debilitating schizophrenia. Because the onset of the disease typically occurs during late adolescence and early adulthood, schizophrenia can often begin distorting the afflicted person's perceptions during the tender early years of social and vocational development.[1] Sometimes, this can result in progress and development that becomes so stunted that the patient is left with mental capacities similar to that of a young child.

But this is not always the case with schizophrenics, of course. One of many notable exceptions would include John Nash, the famous American mathematician who, in spite of the development of schizophrenia around the time he learned that his wife, Alecia, had become pregnant, went on to receive a Nobel Memorial Prize in Economic Sciences in 1994. In a brief autobiography he penned at the time, later appearing in the Nobel Foundation's yearbook publication *Les Prix Nobel,* Nash seemed to hint at the fact that his recovery from schizophrenic hallucinations actually hindered his otherwise brilliant thought processes, claiming that "rationality of thought imposes a limit on a person's concept of his relation to the cosmos."[2]

Such was also the case with one of the patients who had taken residence at the clinic my reader described in her letter. "Anna," a university graduate who had served as a nurse prior to her own diagnosis with schizophrenia, was described as a very gentle, kind, and highly intelligent individual who had remained capable of assisting as a night nurse in the hospital area of the psychiatric center, despite the fact that she was also in treatment for her own condition. During her shifts, Anna began to record the various observations she made of the patients she came into contact with. Predictably, some of these reports verged on the hallucinatory—for example, Anna described encounters with strange beings. Thus, it came to pass that a former staff member from the clinic, now living in Cyprus, took the time to contact me about Anna's observations. Rather candidly she expressed her conviction that some of the things that Anna had described in her reports were the result of *external* influences—perhaps of the spiritual variety—which Anna had somehow been able to perceive.

Though I was unable to engage my contact in further correspondence on the matter, a seed had been planted nonetheless. I soon began to consider the notion—however irrational it may have seemed initially—that perhaps contact with spirits had indeed resulted from (or had been made possible through) Anna's affliction. The implications of this statement may be shocking for some; others may easily dismiss it, asserting instead that Anna's "spirit contact" was merely the by-product of her schizophrenic hallucinations. Admittedly this is what I thought initially, too; however, as I began uncovering other similar cases, my skepticism reverted once again to shock and amazement, and I was finally convinced that the story related by my contact in Cyprus was not the first time a schizophrenic had had some form of paranormal contact.

The late Dr. Wilson Van Dusen was a clinical psychologist and author who devoted the majority of his professional career to learning about schizophrenia. In his essay "The Presence of Spirits in Madness: A Confirmation of Swedenborg in Recent Empirical Findings," Van Dusen recounted how many of the schizophrenics he had worked with throughout the years appeared to behave in a rational, coherent manner, outside of the hallucinations afflicting them. In his studies with these patients, Van Dusen claimed he was able interact with not just the people afflicted with schizophrenia, but also with the *hallucinations* they were describing to him. This interaction seemed to result from the careful manner in which Van Dusen attempted to treat the hallucinations as though they were real, just as his patients believed them to be. His intention had been primarily to put his patients at ease in an environment free of skepticism and related feelings of scorn. Instead, the astonishing result was that he succeeded in noting a number of instances where the information imparted by the "hallucinations" seemed to exceed the level of intellect and knowledge displayed by the patient him- or herself. It was almost as though information Van Dusen received, with its deep spiritual and symbolic overtones, had arrived from some external source of profound intelligence. Not surprisingly, Van Dusen's patients each claimed they were in contact with "another world or order of beings."[3]

Modern psychiatry and pharmacology posit that schizophrenia is likely the result of various chemical imbalances in the brain, with contributing factors ranging from genetics and neurobiology to external psychological influences.[4] But does this exclude the possibility that there might be conditions—chemical or otherwise—that affect the human physiology in ways that allow for a kind of heightened perception that bypasses or exceeds the traditional five senses? What if this perception included beings from other worlds or even spirits of the dead?

Another odd circumstance that seemed to support this idea was shared with me some time ago by the family of a Bulgarian woman named Nadejda. Renowned for her natural beauty, Nadejda had worked for years as a successful runway model, before falling ill due to complications caused by a bacterial infection. Sadly, the infection eventually claimed the life of the promising young talent, but according to the family member who told me Nadejda's story, it had been a life riddled with strange supernatural occurrences. Nadejda had often claimed that she was able to see ghosts and "shadow people," and that these beings interacted with her in various capacities. Once, while visiting a European psychic/fortune teller with friends, she had been disappointed to learn upon arrival that she wouldn't be allowed into the building along with the others. The psychic, who seemed startled, said it was because of "what she was bringing with her," claiming knowledge of dark spiritual energies he believed were surrounding Nadejda. It was later revealed that Nadejda suffered from a form of psychosis, which some doctors and family members had guessed could have been related to a thyroid condition she had developed early on (this condition was also the cause of the infection that ended up taking her life). Therefore, despite the dire testimony of the fortune teller, it could easily be assumed that many of Nadejda's claims had stemmed from within her own mind. This would seem to be a logical conclusion, if it weren't for one particularly striking instance of supernatural intervention to which Nadejda was not the only witness.

The incident in question had taken place only hours after Nadejda's grandmother had passed away. Nadejda had been staying at her family home and was alone at the time, except for a maid who was on duty. Her family was out that evening, and upon returning home, discovered her in a panicked state, standing rooted to the ground and barely able to speak. As her loved ones gathered around, Nadejda's uncle, a physician, went to work trying to learn what might have terrified the girl so badly. After several minutes, she finally regained her composure, explaining that while the family had been gone, someone had called the house phone line. "It was from grandmother," Nadejda insisted, still shaken by the incident—but of course this was impossible, as her grandmother had only recently passed away! Just then, the maid on duty was discovered nearby, weeping in the kitchen. When questioned about the incident, she maintained that what Nadejda had told the rest of the family was accurate, explaining how at the moment the ghostly phone call arrived, she had been standing only a few feet away and overheard the entire conversation as it transpired.

Among Bulgarian funeral traditions, it is common for an informal, second memorial service to occur for the deceased 40 days after the initial wake. Though this is intended to set aside a period of mourning for living relatives, it is also believed that during this time the spirit of the departed may continue to reside in the realm of the living. Thus, it is not uncommon for family members to do things such as leave an open seat at the table where dinner is served so that the spectral visitor will still feel welcome among their earthly kin. Sometimes it is even recommended that family members continue speaking to the deceased so that they will feel that their presence has been acknowledged. Could Nadejda's grandmother have gone to greater lengths to establish contact with her family, knowing that the girl was somehow uniquely predisposed for communication with the dead?

In terms of someone having a sort of "predisposition" toward communication with the dead, as Nadejda did, as well as its potential relationship to psychosis, it is interesting to note that certain substances that are produced in minute quantities within the human body have strong psychoactive properties: namely, DMT and adrenochrome. The latter of these two lie at the heart of a theory for the cause of schizophrenia, as proposed by psychiatrists Abram Hoffer and Humphry Osmond. Their adrenochrome hypothesis involves the administration of large doses of vitamin C and niacin that, as far back as 1967, they had claimed would reduce adrenochrome production in the brain, thus eliminating psychotic delusions.[5] And yet, in terms of its use as a hallucinogen, it is still debated whether adrenochrome has any psychoactive properties that could be considered noteworthy. Many who have experienced its effects describe only mildly strange sensations, akin to numbness in parts of the body, the onset of a mild euphoria, and slight visual distortions, all of which are rather short lived.[6] Nonetheless, its reputation as a powerful hallucinogen has seemed to persist, primarily due to references to its use in the fictional works of American writer Hunter S. Thompson.[7] Whether his descriptions were based in fact or not (it is widely recognized that Thompson had experimented to some degree with virtually every drug he encountered), Thompson's description of the effects of adrenochrome are likened to those of mescaline, including a rise in body temperature and temporary paralysis. In spite of the debate over its *actual* hallucinatory properties, adrenochrome's role in the study of schizophrenic hallucinations remains a point of interest for many in psychiatric circles.

On the other hand, dimethyltryptamine, often referred to simply as DMT, is known to have intense hallucinatory properties. Perhaps the most interesting and controversial aspect of DMT involves reports of contact with otherworldly beings and, on occasion, near-death experiences (NDEs), as documented famously in Dr. Rick Strassman's book *DMT: The Spirit Molecule*. In terms of any potential association between DMT and psychosis, studies that sought to understand psychotic hallucinations and their simi-larities to psychedelics began as early as the 1950s, and, as one might expect, a number of these studies involved the administra-tion of DMT to schizophrenic patients.[8] Additionally, though DMT is synthesized naturally within the human body, as adrenochrome is, it reliably maintains its powerful psychedelic properties when administered under almost all other circumstances, thus leaving little doubt about its potency. Furthermore, Strassman and other researchers who have studied the effects of DMT have questioned whether an *endogenous release* (that is, an amount of DMT released naturally within the body) could be the chemical cause of near-death experiences, mystical states, and a host of other supernatu-ral phenomena.

In a DEA-approved study Strassman performed in the 1990s at the University of New Mexico, a number of participants described entering states that were similar to classic NDEs while under the influence of DMT. Two participants also claimed to have had full-blown NDEs, while a number of others described entering bizarre environments populated with weird machines and buzzing sounds, and inhabited by strange alien beings (note the similarity here to the classic alien abduction scenario). Most of the participants, the majority of whom were experienced past users of psychedelic sub-stances, argued that the beings they saw, rather than having the characteristics of a hallucination, seemed very real. In this sense, the effects of DMT were described by the participants as being much different than those brought about by other substances. And then there were the curious circumstances involving one individu-al who, having been a regular practitioner of meditation, claimed to have achieved a psychedelic state in the past *without* the use of hallucinogens. To Strassman's amazement, this subject did not re-port any psychedelic effects after being administered DMT, thus supporting the notion that some people may be capable of learning how to control and regulate certain metabolic processes within their bodies. If it was theoretically possible to achieve this with regard to endogenous DMT production, it may explain the participant's apparent immunity to DMT's effects.

Again, taking into consideration the fact that DMT is produced within the human body (possibly in the pineal gland), one cannot help but question whether it is intended to serve some greater biological purpose. Assuming this is true, what if some people were more likely than others to have small but potent amounts of DMT released into their bodies? Or, through the cultivation of techniques such as meditation, could it be that some people are teaching themselves how to achieve this over time? Those who claim to have psychic abilities often say that others can fine-tune or ramp up their perception of the spirit world by practicing meditation. This same practice might also enable one to gain control over certain chemical functions in the body, perhaps even the regulation of DMT production. It would be easy to dismiss this as people training or conditioning their minds to perceive hallucinations; but if we suspend our disbelief long enough to consider the outrageous alternative—that those "hallucinations" might sometimes represent external manifestations (spirits and the like)—we might argue that modern scientific institutions, which so often seek to explain away claims of the supernatural as psychotic hallucinations, aren't always accurate in this regard. In other words, could it be that the subtle balance of chemicals that govern the functions of our mind also regulates our perceptions of other realms and even ghosts?

New Zealand psychiatrist Dr. Karl Jansen, through his research into the possible causes of NDEs, seemed to arrive at a similar conclusion, complete with his own hypothesis for chemical causes behind such experiences. In his groundbreaking paper "The Ketamine Model of the Near Death Experience: A Central Role for the NMDA Receptor," Jansen probed the causal relationship between classic

NDE experiences and a multitude of ailments, including conditions such as temporal lobe epilepsy and serotonin imbalances. However, the crux of Jansen's study revealed striking similarities between traditional NDE experiences and the effects of the drug Ketamine, used primarily today as an anesthetic, but also known for having hallucinogenic effects. Jansen discussed at length his observations of how Ketamine "can reproduce all features of the NDE, including travel through a dark tunnel into light, the conviction that one is dead, 'telepathic communion with God,' hallucinations, out-of-body experiences and mystical states." [9] Also of particular interest, Jansen notes that Ketamine, "if given intravenously...has a short action with an abrupt end."[10] This description is reminiscent of DMT's effects on the human physiology, which are often described as fleeting but very intense (many liken it to being fired from a cannon).

Though Jansen's initial studies with Ketamine point to a physiological basis for NDEs, his views regarding their cause, as well as his interpretation of NDEs in general, seemed to change over time. Following the publication of the results of his Ketamine studies, Jansen made note of this change, apparently welcoming further correspondence from those who shared his beliefs:

> I am no longer as opposed to spiritual explanations of these phenomena as this article would appear to suggest. Over the past two years...I have moved more towards the view...that drugs and psychological disciplines such as meditation and yoga may render certain "states" more accessible.

Jansen further commented on the mysterious states that appear to be aroused by the onset of Ketamine's hallucinogenic effects:

> The complication then becomes in defining just what we mean by "states" and where they are located, if

indeed location is an appropriate term at all. But the apparent emphasis on matter over mind contained within this particular article no longer accurately represents my attitudes. My forthcoming book *Ketamine* will consider mystical issues from quite a different perspective, and will give a much stronger voice to those who see drugs as just another door to a space, and not as actually producing that space.[11]

Science continues to ponder whether there could be some causative connection between hallucinations and their biological causes on one hand, and supernatural encounters with ghosts and the afterlife on the other. In spite of the fact that the evidence says that there is, the implications of this fact nonetheless stand in opposition to the more conventional interpretations of paranormal phenomena at the hands of modern science. The main problem is the disjointed manner in which science relates the curious pieces of the greater puzzle as they are uncovered; the left hand knows not what the right hand is doing. Little more can be said of the multitude of scientific branches that continuously fail (or, more probably, refuse) to share information with one another. This doesn't need to be our fate, however. If an analytical psychologist's perspective on a matter of spirit manifestation were brought together and compared with the research of a pharmacologist colleague studying the effects of hallucinogens on the mind, who knows what fascinating parallels might be brought to the forefront? Of course, this is not to say that interdisciplinary studies *never* occur; but they need to occur more often. Otherwise, relatively common "paranormal" phenomena such as sleep paralysis, ghostly encounters, and glimpses of life after death may continue to be quickly "diagnosed" as singular, troublesome psychotic breaks with reality, based simply on a one-dimensional perspective that would seek to classify them as "abnormal" at all costs.

It is worth noting here that even in many indigenous cultures and traditions around the world, clear distinctions are drawn between those who are mentally unstable and those who claim to have some perception of or interaction with the supernatural world. Psychologist Jane Murphy found that both the Inuit and West African Yoruba separate those suffering from mental illness from those who claim to have shamanic abilities. The Inuit word *nuth-kavihak*, for instance, describes "a person who carries on conversations with himself or who refuses to speak at all."[12] The Yoruba have a word with almost identical meaning, *were*; both of these terms are used to describe what modern psychiatrists would likely classify as psychotic behavior.[13]

Though indigenous societies draw the necessary distinctions between mental illness and supernatural abilities, perhaps the boundaries that separate the two are less clear-cut than originally thought. Perhaps many of the same biological conditions in our bodies that, in extreme cases, escalate into diseases such as schizophrenia, are, when properly regulated, also the means by which we perceive otherworldly phenomena. Of course, this begs the question of whether it will ever be possible for us to draw the line between a psychic gift and a psychotic nightmare. Thus, we are presented with unsteady ground for future research; after all, taking on an ultimate understanding of strange phenomena, the workings of the human mind, and how the two may be interrelated may force us to redefine reality itself. Despite humanity's best efforts throughout the centuries, this singular quest has proved to be the most elusive. The greatest mystery of all is comprised of those things we see each and every day around us, yet which we cannot *know* in the truest sense of the word, beyond the inner walls of our craniums. What if, as so many philosophers and thinkers of ages past have already suggested, everything were merely an illusion? And furthermore, if this were true, how would an encounter with a ghost or spirit be any different from shaking your neighbor's hand when you meet him on the street? Perhaps this is the key to the great mystery of the unexplained. If we truly understood the inner workings of the human mind, we would likely realize that the supernatural is, in truth, quite natural, and that the many instances of strange phenomena that have continued to baffle us represent things that *do actually exist*—inasmuch as you or I could be said to exist with any degree of certainty.

Notes

1. Cullen K.R., S. Kumra, J. Regan, M. Westerman, C. Schulz, "Atypical Antipsychotics for Treatment of Schizophrenia Spectrum Disorders," *Psychiatric Times* (March 1, 2008).

2. Nash, John, *Autobiography From Les Prix Nobel*. Ed. Tore Frängsmyr (Stockholm: Nobel Foundation, 1995).

3. Van Dusen, Wilson Miles, *The Presence of Spirits in Madness* (New York: The Swedenborg Foundation, 1972).

4. Colburn, Rebekah, "Understanding Schizophrenia: The Basics. Schizophrenia Causes, Symptoms, Therapy and Statistics." Accessed November 24, 2010. *http://www.suite101.com/content/understanding-schizophrenia---brain-disorder-a214502*.

5. Hoffer, A. and H. Osmond, *The Hallucinogens* (New York: Academic Press, 1967).

6. Erowid Adrenochrome Vault. Accessed November 21, 2010. *http://www.erowid.org/chemicals/adrenochrome/adrenochrome.shtml*.

7. Thompson, Hunter S., *Fear and Loathing in Las Vegas: A Savage Journey to the Heart of the American Dream* (New York: Popular Library, 1971).

8. Strassman, Rick, *DMT: the Spirit Molecule: A Doctor's Revolutionary Research into the Biology of Near-Death and Mystical Experiences* (Rochester, Vt.: Park Street, 2001).

9. Jansen, Dr. Karl L. R., *The Ketamine Model of the Near Death Experience: A Central Role for the NMDA Receptor* Springer, Netherlands: *Journal of Near-Death Studies* 16, no. 1 (Fall 1997).

10. Ibid.

11. Jansen, Dr. Karl L. R. "Near Death Experiences." Accessed November 23, 2010. *http://www.mindspring.com/~scottr/nde/jansen1.html.*

12. Murphy, J.M. "Psychiatric labeling in cross-cultural perspective." *Science* (March 1976): 191, 1019–1028.

13. Ibid.

Monsters of the Spectral Kind

By Nick Redfern

When, with my teenage years looming, I became seriously fascinated by the subject of cryptozoology—the search for and study of mysterious, undocumented creatures such as Sasquatch, the Yeti, and the Loch Ness Monster—everything for me was very much black-and-white: Bigfoot and the Abominable Snowman were giant, as-yet-unclassified apes; the Loch Ness Monsters (I use the plural here because encounters have spanned more than a thousand years, indicating that there is likely more than one creature) were surviving relics from the Jurassic era; and the veritable menagerie of other amazing animals in our midst, including werewolves and sea-serpents, were simply creatures that science and zoology had yet to definitively classify. Unknown or not, they were still flesh-and-blood creatures—or so I assumed. As time progressed, however, and as my 'teens became my twenties and then my thirties, my views began to change, and with very good reason. The beasts with which I had become obsessed as a child, I later came to realize, were not just strange: they were actually *too* strange.

Elusive Creatures

Despite the fact that there have been literally thousands of sightings of Bigfoot within the dark forests of North America over the past several centuries, all attempts to identify, trap, or kill even one such animal have ended in complete and utter failure. Unlike just about every other living creature in the United States, Bigfoot has never had the misfortune of being hit by a car or truck and killed, nor has anyone ever stumbled across a corpse of one of these elusive animals. And there are countless cases on record in which people have attempted to shoot Bigfoot, but the bullets seem to have no effect on the animals whatsoever. It's much the same with the monsters of Loch Ness, Scotland. Although the Loch is sizeable—it is approximately 24 miles long, roughly a mile wide, and about 700 feet deep—it is hardly remote or inaccessible. Certainly, every year, tens of thousands of people flock to Scotland in the hope of seeing the shy, long-necked entities of those dark waters, and nearly all go home disappointed. Ambitious projects designed to seek out the creatures with sonar and submarines have always failed to turn up anything conclusive. Attempts to photograph the animals, on the rare occasions they have surfaced from the murky depths, have often proved to be curiously problematic, as well: cameras jam at crucial moments, and photographs are inexplicably blurred or fogged.

Then there's the matter of the eating habits of these mysterious beasts—or, more correctly, their overwhelming *lack* of eating habits. Bigfoot, given its immense size and build (eyewitness reports describe a creature eight feet tall and weighing an estimated 300 to 600 pounds), would likely require a massive intake of food on a daily basis. After all, a fully grown silverback gorilla requires 45 pounds of food per day on average—and that's just for one animal. Imagine the amount of nourishment required by a whole colony of silverbacks! Indeed, one of the reasons why it is so easy to track the movements and activities of gorillas is not only because they are very social animals that live in groups, but also because of the clear and undeniable evidence of their massive, hour-by-hour efforts foraging for food. However, there is very little, if any, evidence of Bigfoot's culinary exploits. Yes, there are very occasional reports of Bigfoot killing a pig here or a deer there, but for the most part the hard evidence of its eating habits—which, again, would have to be tremendous in scope—is conspicuously absent. Moreover, that Bigfoot is seen in locales hardly noted for their rich and abundant food supplies, such as the depths of the Nevada desert and West Texas, only adds to the high strangeness.

And it's much the same with Loch Ness: if a large colony of plesiosaurs has managed to survive extinction and now calls the Loch their home, how, exactly, are they sustaining their massive bulk? Yes, the Loch is populated by a number of kinds of fish, such as salmon, eel, pike, and trout, but the populations are most assuredly not in the numbers that would allow a school of 20 aquatic beasts, each 15 to 25 feet in length, to secure sufficient nourishment on a day-to-day basis to ensure their survival, health, and reproduction over the centuries. In other words, while most, if not all of the many and varied creatures that fall squarely under the cryptozoological banner appear at first glance to be flesh-and-blood animals—albeit ones as-yet unclassified by science—upon careful study, their curious eating habits and activities suggest they are actually nothing of the sort. Indeed, given their elusiveness, they seem rather more spectral, ethereal, and phantom-like in nature. Could it be the case that some of the strange and fantastic monsters that plague and perplex people all across the world on dark, windswept nights, within thick woods, and amid the cold waters of ancient lakes are far less—or, paradoxically, far more—than they appear to be? Are our monsters actually ghosts? Let's take a careful look at the evidence. We'll begin with a diabolical, glowing-eyed creature that still haunts the old, winding waterways of central England.

The Phantom Beast of the Canal

On the chilly evening of January 21, 1879, a man was walking home, with his horse and cart in tow, along the tree-shrouded lanes that to this day still link the hamlet of Woodcote in Shropshire to the tiny locale of Ranton, Staffordshire, England. All was as it should be until around 10 p.m. when, barely a mile from Woodscaves and while crossing over Bridge 39 on the Shropshire Union Canal, the man was suddenly plunged into chaos and terror. Out of the darkened woods emerged a frightening beast: it was large, black-haired, and monkey-like in appearance, with a pair of brightly illumi-nated eyes that glowed eerily and hypnotically.

The monster suddenly jumped atop the cart and then, incred-ibly, leapt onto the back of the terrified horse, which took off in a frenzied gallop with the cart careening wildly behind. The man, to his credit, gave chase, and finally caught up with the horse, cart, and beast. He then proceeded to hit with his whip what was sure-ly the closest thing the British Isles have ever seen to Bigfoot. The man later reported that each time he tried to strike the beast, the whip simply passed through its body, as though the hairy thing were nothing less than a terrifying specter of the night. A moment later, and without warning, the creature leapt to the ground and bounded away into the safety of the dark woods that loomed on both sides. The shocking event was over as quickly as it had begun.

Racing to a local pub for a much-needed pint of beer (or sev-eral), the man, in shaky tones, told his story to the astounded and worried customers and staff. He then headed back home and took to his bed, where he reportedly spent two days in a state of near-exhaustion. Soon, the local police got wind of the story, who duly told the eyewitness's employer that the existence of the beast was well-known in the area. Dubbed the Man-Monkey, the police said, it had first surfaced from the woods surrounding the canal after a man had died upon falling into its cold, dark waters late one night, some months earlier. It is intriguing to note that the local police linked the beginnings of the Man-Monkey legend with the death of a man who had drowned in the Shropshire Union Canal. In some areas of Britain that still held to ancient traditions and folklore, it was widely believed at the time that the souls of recently departed people could return to the material plane of existence in the form of horrific beasts—beasts of a type that would fit quite comfortably within the realm of today's field of cryptozoology.

Charlotte S. Burne, a writer who, in the late 1800s, became fascinated by the legend of the Man-Monkey, outlined the nature of the beliefs relative to "the constant transformation of the departed into animals" (Burne 1883). She wrote:

> I believe this to have originated in the classical and medieval notion of werewolves, living men who could assume the shape of a wolf at pleasure. Sometimes also a corpse would arise from its grave in the form of a wolf, and might do incalculable damage if it were not at once beheaded and cast into the nearest stream. Wolves have been extinct in England long enough to have disappeared from popular tales, though not so many centuries as most people suppose, but the Man-Monkey seems very like the old fable in a new guise (Ibid).

And there is another aspect to the saga of the Man-Monkey that also places the beast in a definitively paranormal realm that is suggestive of a link to the afterlife. On December 8, 1878—only a month before the Man-Monkey manifested on Bridge 39 of the Shropshire Union Canal—*Sheldrake's Aldershot & Sandhurst Military Gazette* reported on the rumor that a gorilla had been seen in the area on several occasions, reportedly having escaped from a traveling menagerie only a short distance from the canal bridge where the Man-Monkey had appeared. Was the story true? Was there really a mobile zoo from which a gorilla had made a successful bid for freedom? And if so, did it briefly make its home in the wilds of Shropshire and bordering Staffordshire before succumbing to

Bridge 39 on England's Shropshire Union Canal, the lair of the Man-Monkey.
Copyright Nick Redfern.

starvation and the effects of a harsh English winter, before return-ing in ghostly form to haunt Bridge 39? If the Man-Monkey really was some form of spectral entity, such a theory might very well explain why sightings of the terrible creature have continued to be reported as late as 2008. After all, it's well-nigh impossible that a solitary creature could roam the area for 130 years and never be caught, let alone live for such an astonishingly long period of time. It seems very likely that Britain's Bigfoot is a beast of a definitively supernatural nature.

Ghostly Black Dogs

There is another creature that dominates British-based cryp-tozoological research that also seems to have a link to the realm of the recently departed. For centuries, the ghostly Black Dog, or Devil Dog, has been an integral part of British folklore and mythol-ogy as well as the world of monster-hunting. Generally described as being much larger than any normal hound, its coat is utterly black, its eyes blaze like fiery, red-hot coals, and its appearance and presence is often perceived as an ominous portent of disaster, tragedy, and death. In other words, the Black Dog of Britain is the grim reaper in animal form. It has also been suggested that this monster represents the spectral form of the dead returned.

London's Newgate Jail was the location of an encounter with just such a creepy critter centuries ago. One Luke Hutton, a crimi-nal who had been executed at the English city of York in the late 1590s, described the event in a pamphlet that was not published until 1812, years after his death. Titled *The Discovery of a London Monster, called the black dog of Newgate*, Hutton's story suggested that a marauding, glowing-eyed black hound that was seen prowl-ing around the jail was actually the ghost of a scholar who had been imprisoned in Newgate, and who had subsequently been killed and eaten by the starving inmates. He had returned in monstrous, dog-like form to exact his revenge on those who had so violently ended his life.

Then there is the very weird tale of William and David Sutor. The dark saga all began late one night in December of 1728, when William, a Scottish farmer, was hard at work in his fields when he heard an unearthly shriek that was accompanied by a brief glimpse of a large, dark-colored dog, far bigger than any normal hound and possessing a pair of the ubiquitous, glowing eyes. And on several more occasions from 1729 to 1730, the dog returned, always seemingly intent on plaguing the Sutor family. In late November of 1730, the affair reached its paranormal pinnacle.

Once again, the mysterious dog manifested before the farmer, but this time, incredibly, it spoke in rumbling tones, directing William to make his way to a nearby area within 30 minutes. William, naturally, did as he was told, and there waiting for him was the spectral hound. The terrified William pleaded to know what was going on. The hound answered that it was none other than David Sutor, William's brother. It went on to say that he had killed a man at that very spot some 35 years earlier. Just as David had directed his own

An ancient text describing Britain's ghostly black Devil Dogs. From Abraham Fleming's *A Straunge and Terrible Wunder*, published by J. Compton Publishers, London, 1820.

savage dog to kill the man, he, David, had been returned to our plane of existence in the form of a gigantic hound as punishment. The black hound instructed William to seek out the buried bones of the murdered man and then place them within consecrated ground, which William duly did, in the confines of the old Blair Churchyard. The ghostly black dog—the spirit of David Sutor in

An 18th-century engraving of Newgate Prison, London—
the haunt of a glowing-eyed, monstrous hound.

animalistic, spectral form—vanished, and was reportedly never seen nor heard from again. In this case, the presence of the hound did not presage death, but, as the tale demonstrates, it was intimately connected with the domain of the dead. Although the image that the Devil Dog conjures up is that of a sinister beast prowling the villages and hamlets of centuries-old England, sightings of such creatures have continued until relatively recent times.

Interestingly, one area that seems to attract more than its fair share of such encounters is a sprawling mass of dense forest in Staffordshire, England, known as the Cannock Chase. Indeed, among the folk of the many small villages that either sit on the fringes of the Chase or are found deep within the heart of its wooded depths, tales of the vile hounds of hell are disturbingly and surprisingly common. It appears that the traditions and beliefs of old are still at work in modern times. In one such tale, late one evening in early 1972, a man named Nigel Lea was driving across the Cannock Chase when his attention was suddenly drawn to a strange ball of glowing, blue light that appeared to slam into the ground some distance ahead of his vehicle amid a veritable torrent of bright, fiery sparks. Needless to say, Lea quickly slowed his car down, and as he approached the area where he had seen the light fall, he was shocked and horrified to see looming before him "the biggest bloody dog I have ever seen in my life" (Redfern, 2001). Muscular and black, with large, pointed ears and huge paws, the creature seemed to positively ooze malice and menace, and had a wild, staring look in its yellow-tinged eyes. For about 30 seconds, man and beast faced each other, after which time the animal slowly and cautiously headed for the tall trees and finally disappeared, never once taking its penetrating eyes off the petrified driver. Somewhat ominously, and around two or three weeks later, says Lea, a close friend of his was killed in an industrial accident under horrific circumstances in the town of West Bromwich. After having deeply studied the history of Black Dog lore, Lea believes this event was somehow connected to his strange encounter on that tree-shrouded road back in 1972.

Lake-Monster Specters

And what about Britain's most famous monster, Nessie? What do the experts say about this elusive creature? While digging deep into the subject of the U.S. government's secret research into the realms of so-called remote viewing and psychic spying, Jim Marrs, one of the world's leading experts on conspiracy theories, learned that officials once attempted to solve the riddle of what it is that lurks within Loch Ness in Scotland by using these so-called psi spies. However, as Marr's noted, it was no easy task. Several remote viewing sessions that targeted the Loch Ness Monster, said Marrs, actually revealed physical traces of the beast, such as a wake in the water or the distinct movement of a large body beneath the surface of the Loch. Significantly, those involved in the remote viewing even made drawings of long-necked, hump-backed animals that eerily resembled the presumed-extinct plesiosaurs of the Jurassic era. As Marrs noted, however, when the government's remote viewers attempted to dig further into the puzzle, they hit upon a startling discovery: the creatures—if that is what they were—seemed to have the ability to appear and vanish into thin air, just like the classic, chain-rattling spirits of yore, one might argue. According to Marrs, "considering that reports of human ghosts date back throughout man's history, the psi spies seriously considered the possibility that the Loch Ness Monster is nothing less than a dinosaur's ghost" (Marrs 2007).

And with these tales of the paranormal monsters of the British Isles in mind, let us take a trip across the pond to the United States.

Beast-Men, Ghost Lights, and Indian Souls

The Big Thicket truly lives up to its name. An 83,000-acre area of East Texas's Piney Woods, it is a sprawling mass of rivers, swampland, and incredibly dense forests comprised of cypress trees, short-leaf pines, and huge oaks and beech trees. The Big Thicket is also home to a whole host of beasts, including armadillos, alligators, panthers, bobcats, and an array of snakes.

Interestingly, today, the Big Thicket is said to be home to nothing less than the Lone Star State equivalent of Bigfoot—and a spectral Bigfoot, no less. Bragg Road, or Ghost Road, as it is known locally, is where most of the action occurs. It is situated right in the heart of the Big Thicket, and begins at a bend on Farm-to-Market Road 787 that is just a short distance from Saratoga. Ghost Road takes its name from the fact that the surrounding area is populated by eerie, floating balls of light which, for decades, have been seen flitting in and around the darkened woods. Explanations for these "ghost lights" are varied and colorful. Some people believe they are merely the reflections of car headlamps, while the scientific community believes they are caused by gaseous substances emanating from the swamps. Some suggest that the lights are similar to the famous Marfa lights (also of Texas), while there are also those theorists who muse upon the possibility that the Bragg Road lights are indicative of an ongoing UFO presence in the area. More than a few researchers have wondered if the ghost lights are the wandering souls of the Native Americans that dwelled in the depths of the Big Thicket centuries ago.

It is against this curious backdrop of ghostly lights in the sky and tales of discarnate Indian souls that the Texas Bigfoot has time and again put in an appearance. One such story came to me a number of years ago from someone I'll call Gerald, a no-nonsense individual who had worked in a Port Arthur, Texas refinery for years, and who lived a short journey from the town of Kountze, which is surrounded by the Big Thicket. According to Gerald, his

Are the creatures of the deep flesh-and-blood or spectral? From *The Search for the Giant Squid* by Richard Ellis, published by Lyons Press in 1998.

encounter occurred in June 1977, interestingly enough, around the "witching hour," when he was driving through Kountze and near the town's Old Hardin Cemetery. Suddenly, his car's engine began to falter and its lights faded. Gerald, thinking that perhaps a blown fuse was to blame, carefully brought the vehicle to a halt at the side of the road. However, as he exited the vehicle to take a look under the hood, at a distance of perhaps 50 or 60 feet, Gerald saw a tall, skinny, bipedal, hirsute figure walking across the road. The sighting only lasted a few seconds, and the creature vanished—literally into thin air—as it reached the trees at the edge of the road. But most notable was what happened next: only two or three seconds later, a soccer ball–sized glowing mass of bright light came floating through the trees at a height of about 50 or 60 feet, and from the exact spot where the creature had vanished into the woods. The ghost light moved slowly across the road until it was lost from sight amid the thick trees on the opposite side. Interestingly, after both the beast and the light had vanished, Gerald's car started normally and never showed signs of any similar problem again.

Welcome to the Big Thicket! Copyright Nick Redfern.

A similar story was brought to my attention by a man whom I will call Will, who had seen a large and lumbering ape-like creature crossing the road near the Big Thicket's Bragg Road late at night, in the winter of 1978. Will described the beast as being around 7 feet tall, jet-black in color, and with a head that sat squarely on its shoulders. He added that the creature moved slowly across the road and swung its arms as it did so, but did not appear fazed or at all concerned by the fact that the headlights of Will's car illuminated its face. In a situation that eerily parallels some of the more mysterious cryptozoological encounters on record, when Will came within about 50 yards of the creature, the engine and headlights on his car both failed. It was only when the creature seemed to disappear in a flash of light as it walked to the edge of the woods that Will was able to restart his vehicle. As a result of this encounter, he became a firm believer in the theory that the Big Thicket wild man is some form of paranormal entity, rather than a flesh-and-blood animal.

A Spectral Werewolf

More recently, paranormal expert Joshua P. Warren told me that he had extensively investigated a series of encounters with apparitional monsters on farmland at Lancaster, South Carolina—one of which was a spectral winged terror that seemed to resemble nothing less than a pterodactyl. But in order to take a look at one of the most bizarre stories that Warren has ever investigated, we must turn our attention to the case of the ghostly werewolf. As Warren himself told me,"This story blew my mind. It came from a woman whose property was being haunted by wolf-like animals. She went to sleep one night and woke up in the middle of the night. Standing next to her was this huge, ghostly, wolfman-type figure. It was large and tall, and she was instantly horrified. When she locked eyes with [it], she was petrified and couldn't move" (Redfern 2008).

Phantom werewolves on the prowl. From *The Werewolf Delusion* by Ian Woodward, published by Paddington Press, 1979.

The woman told Warren that she immediately intuited that the werewolf wanted one thing and one thing only: sex. Warren adds: "She quickly rolled over and hid under the covers, with her heart pounding. She thought the covers would be ripped away from her and she would become his little sex toy. But he quickly vanished from the room" (Ibid.). Warren has an interesting theory to account for such sexually themed stories involving monstrous animals: "I've always wondered if these creatures could be energy-vampires—not necessarily men or women or crypto-monsters, at all, but more like *incubi* and *succubi* creatures that have been reported for thousands of years. Whereas we might eat meat and vegetables for energy, they are paranormal creatures from the afterlife that come into your room in the middle of the night and take energy via sex" (Ibid.).

Of course, as fascinating as such tales are, they are all dependent on three things: that there is an afterlife, that animals have souls, and that those same animals are able to return in some ghost-like form. Given that Warren has investigated a number of cryptozoological cases, and given that he is also the author of *Pet Ghosts*, he—perhaps more than anyone else in the ghost-hunting community—is in a prime position to comment on such matters. When I interviewed Warren in 2008 regarding these cases, he told me that the phenomenon seemed to be multifaceted.

Paranormal expert Joshua P. Warren. Copyright Nick Redfern.

Warren believes that there are several different types of animal ghosts. The most obvious ones are those that had once existed in the physical realm but had attained some form of continued life in the realm of the dead. Such an animal ghost, Warren explains, may be self-aware. The spirit of a much-loved pet that returns to comfort its distraught owners and demonstrate that physical death is not the end is a perfect example, he says. Then, there are those animal ghosts that seem to wholly lack any form of self-awareness, such as a phantom horse seen pulling an equally ghostly stage-coach along the same stretch of road time and time again. Warren suspects that the ghostly, black Devil Dog is in this category, as well, and may have its origins in some dark, ominous realm that has somehow intersected with our own. In other words, calling the strange creatures and monsters of our world "ghosts" is only part of the story. The trick is to figure out precisely which category of ghost each of the respective mysterious animals falls into. Indeed, Warren has seriously considered the possibility that the ghostly presence of certain extinct animals might very well help explain modern-day sightings of monstrous beasts: "Maybe Bigfoot is a *phantimal*," Warren said, using his term for these ghostly beasts, "perhaps...even the ghosts of prehistoric creatures or the spirits of primitive humans" (Ibid.).

Animals, Monsters, Life After Death, and the Government

A U.S. Defense Intelligence Agency document dating from September 1975, titled *Soviet and Czechoslovakian Parapsychological Research*, and which has since been declassified under the terms of the Freedom of Information Act, revealed a wealth of interest on the part of the American military in the research of a Soviet doctor—one Pavel Naumov—as it relates to life-after-death in the animal kingdom. Somewhat disturbingly, the document states in part:

> Dr. Naumov conducted studies between a submerged Soviet Navy submarine and a shore research station: these tests involved a mother rabbit and her newborn litter and occurred around 1956. According to Naumov, Soviet scientists placed the baby rabbits aboard the submarine. They kept the mother rabbit in a laboratory on shore where they implanted electrodes in her brain. When the submarine was submerged, assistants killed the rabbits one by one. At each precise moment of death, the mother rabbit's brain produced detectable and recordable reactions (Maire III 1975).

Far more significantly, American military spies writing in 1975 noted that "[a]s late as 1970 the precise protocol and results of this test described by Naumov were believed to be classified" (Ibid.).

While this official document—once classified as Top Secret and circulated amongst the highest echelons of the defense and intelligence communities—is primarily concerned with the issues of mind-reading and ESP, it is important to note that the Defense Intelligence Agency took careful note of the fact that the mother rabbit in the 1956 experiments clearly reacted at the moment her offspring were killed. At the very least, this suggests that physical death in animals is still not fully understood, and that it may hold further startling surprises for us. A second copy of this document, declassified in 2007 by the National Security Agency, includes a very intriguing, albeit brief, hand-written notation on the document that states the following: "A better understanding of Naumov's work might make our 'Bigfoot' archives clearer. Can Wenner look into this further?" (Ibid.) Despite persistent digging on my part, precisely what the NSA's Bigfoot archives were, and who Wenner was, is very much an ongoing puzzle. However, that someone within the NSA had made a connection between Naumov's work on animal souls and the Bigfoot conundrum is intriguing to say the very least.

Perhaps the government knows something we don't about animals, cryptozoology, and the afterlife. Maybe they are fully aware that the Loch Ness Monster, Bigfoot, werewolves, and those spectral dogs are not the flesh-and-blood creatures they appear to be, but are the dead returned to life in vile, nightmarish, monstrous forms that invade our world, taunt weary travelers, and haunt our dreams as we sleep. Sasquatch, Nessie, and the Yeti—they all exist, of that I have no doubt. But they may be even more loathsome, more terrifying than previously thought. Indeed, this beastly menagerie may collectively represent our absolute worst nightmare come true.

Bibliography

(Note: All Websites were last checked in January of 2011.)

Burne, Charlotte S. and Georgina Jackson. *Shropshire Folklore*. London: Trubner Books, 1883.

"Capturing a Gorilla in Shropshire." *Sheldrake's Aldershot & Sandhurst Military Gazette* (no author credited). December 8, 1878.

Clark, James. *Haunted London*. Stroud, UK: Tempus Publishing, 2007.

Harmsworth, A.J. "Loch Ness Information Website." *http://www. loch-ness.org/*.

Maire III, Louis F. and J.D. LaMothe. *Soviet and Czechoslovakian Parapsychological Research*. Washington, D.C.: Defense Intelligence Agency, 1975.

Marrs, Jim. *Psi Spies*. Franklin Lakes, N.J.: New Page Books, 2007.

National Parks Services, Department of the Interior. "The Big Thicket." *http://www.nps.gov/bith/historyculture/index.htm*. No author given. Accessed September 19, 2006.

Redfern, Nick. Interview with Gerald Ray. June 12, 2005.

———. Interview with Nigel Lea. March 3, 2001.

———. Interviews with Joshua Warren. August 2, 2008 and July 7, 2010.

———. Interview with Will Porter. March 14, 2002.

———. *Man-Monkey: In Search of the British Bigfoot*. Woolsery, UK: CFZ Press, 2007.

Riggs, Rob. *In the Big Thicket*. New York: Paraview Press, 2001.

"The History of Cannock Chase." *http://www.cannockchasehistory. org.uk/index.php*. No author given.

Trubshaw, Bob (ed.). *Explore Phantom Black Dogs*. Loughborough, UK: Heart of Albion Press, 2005.

Urban, Sylvanus. *Gentleman's Magazine or Monthly Intelligencer for the Year 1731*. Vol. 1, F. London: Jeffries Publishers, 1731.

Warren, Joshua P. *Pet Ghosts: Animal Encounters From Beyond the Grave*. Franklin Lakes, N.J.: New Page Books, 2006.

Road Tripping: Phantom Hitchhikers

By Ursula Bielski

In my Chicago, sleeping amid the bustle, cemeteries wait everywhere. In the daylight, they are themselves little cities: slowly concocted metropolises of architecture and art, landscape planning and limestone, names great and small. Though they are, like the neighborhoods that have grown around them, crowded, jaded, and full of secrets, there are mysteries here far beyond those ordinary secrets of the living. At night, between the light and life of intersections urban and remote, the darkness blots out the distinguishing elements of monuments and trees, chapels and mausoleums, transforming them into vast stretches of blackness that run like coastlines along the roads. For centuries, in Chicago and in cities around the world, drivers passing along these cemetery-strewn highways have told of a unique breed of ghost story: that of the "vanishing (or phantom) hitchhiker," a wandering spirit, typically in the form of a beautiful young woman, who thumbs rides in the dead of night, only to vanish from the cars of the shocked Good Samaritan who has offered her a lift.

The legend of the phantom hitchhiker (PH) was and still is a fixture in the ghostlore of my hometown, where as a young girl I first learned of the fascinating phantom known only as Resurrection Mary, arguably the best-known among the countless PHs reported around the globe. For more than 70 years, travelers along Chicgo's Archer Avenue have reported bizarre encounters with a single-minded young woman in a white dress and dancing shoes who seems as real as can be—that is, until she proves to be decidedly otherwise. Mary first appeared to unsuspecting Southwest-side drivers in the mid-1930s, when late-night revelers began complaining to police that a woman had tried to jump on the running boards of their automobiles as they passed Resurrection Cemetery on their way home from the old O. Henry Ballroom. Others driving along Archer in the early hours reported that they had come upon a woman wandering barefoot in the road, wearing a lavish party dress but no coat. Offering her a ride home, she would give vague directions up Archer, only to vanish from the vehicle as it passed the cemetery gates.

Encounters inside the O. Henry Ballroom also were reported, as well as incidents in various other dance halls in the Back of the Yards neighborhood, which many of the stories pinpoint as the center of their tales. These interior encounters also followed a similar story: time and again, a young man would meet a moody young woman, share dances with her, but later describe her as socially "cold" as well as cold to the touch. After these dances, the girl would become panicky and beg for a ride home, but every time, before the couple could reach the destination, she would disappear from the car. A classic version of the story tells of how, after such an incident, the bewildered young man went on to the address given by the girl, only to be told by the residents that she had been dead for years.

As I grew up and became ever more interested in Chicago's ghostlore, I learned that Mary was not the only PH to have crossed paths with a Chicagoan—nor was she even the first. A number of witnesses reported a PH around the time of the Century of Progress Exposition, the World's Fair of 1933, one year before the first sighting of Resurrection Mary. In those accounts, people traveling by car to the Fair are hailed by a woman by the roadside carrying a bag. When the driver picks her up and the traveling party engages her in conversation, the woman begins making bizarre prognostications. She tells them that the fairgrounds are going to slide into Lake Michigan in the coming months, and predicts the exact death dates of each of the passengers. Before they can ask the bizarre passenger to disembark, however, she does them the favor of disappearing. That same year, also predating the Mary sightings, revelers traveling home from the old Melody Mill Ballroom in the suburb of Forest Park were allegedly flagged down by a beautiful young flapper walking along the fence of Waldheim Cemetery. Eager to drive the girl home—and perhaps enjoy a nightcap—her impromptu escort would instead receive the shock of his life. While passing the communal mausoleum, the girl would simply open the car door and run from the moving vehicle and straight *through* the cemetery fence. St. Casimir Cemetery, not far from Resurrection, is also home to the so-called Sneering Stranger, a frightening and forlorn man known to wander the road outside (111th street). And a wayfaring young girl is tied in legend to Evergreen Cemetery, and has even been known to board the bus outside its entrance. When the driver asks for her fare, she claims to be destitute. Attempts to take her home or to the police always fail, however: en route, she mysteriously vanishes.

Far from being indigenous only to Chicago, phantom hitchhikers are an international phenomenon. Nor are they anything new: sightings date as far back as Biblical times. One such sighting tells the story of a man named Philip, who baptizes an Ethiopian who has picked him up in a chariot, only to disappear. Then there are ancient tales from India, Africa, China, South America, and Britain. Often they involve a man traveling on horseback through the countryside who picks up a beautiful woman walking near the road. After mounting the back of the horse and being carried to the next town, the woman simply vanishes before they reach their destination. And ever since the tsunami that devastated Thailand in 2004, stories have circulated of taxi drivers who continue to pick up the wandering dead. Most versions of the tale describe a driver who picks up a couple looking for a ride to the airport in Phuket. When the taxi arrives at the destination, the driver turns around to find that his fare has silently vanished. This commonly retold tale is accompanied by ongoing reports of taxi drivers picking up one or several passengers near the beach, all of whom simply vanish after boarding the cab. But are these apparitions, phantoms, hallucinations, cultural delusions, or something else?

The legend of the vanishing hitchhiker is a tale told widely, but each iteration has its own distinctly local flavor. Though the theme seems to be universal, the particular stories themselves are generally connected to local histories or personalities and thus are part of a community's or region's folklore. This important fact gained much greater recognition with the publication of Jan Harold Brunvand's debut volume of urban legends, *The Vanishing Hitchhiker: American Urban Legends and Their Meanings*. It was only after this volume was released that a non-scholarly audience began to understand the value and meaning of urban legends on a wide scale. However, doubt continued to grow along with this new awareness.

Folklorists such as Brunvand classify PH encounters as urban legends. Folklorists specializing in urban legends do not believe that these encounters are real. According to Brunvand and others, PH stories are merely cautionary tales meant to inspire fear in order to teach some kind of lesson or moral—in this case, "don't pick up hitchhikers" or "don't drive alone at night." Likewise, mental health experts working in Thailand after the 2004 tsunami confidently stated that survivors witnessing alleged phantoms were, in short, delusional. Thai psychologist and media commentator

Wallop Piyamanotham declared to the AFP that survivors were participating in a "mass hallucination that is a cue to the trauma being suffered by people who are missing so many dead people, and seeing so many dead people, and only talking about dead people" (from News.com.au).

This idea of mass hallucination is closer to a longtime theory held by psychologists that "witnesses" to PHs are simply hallucinating. They may think they are seeing a PH, but there is no objective reality to what they are seeing. In this case, the hitchhikers are not ghosts, but illusions induced by both the witnesses' expectations and the hypnogogic effect of night travel along darkened roads. Gently eased into the mildest of hypnotic states by the relaxing effect of a quiet car and a darkened landscape, drivers may find themselves both expressing and easing their disorientation by literally giving form to their fears of isolation by creating a traveling companion. Add to this the presence of a cemetery, and it's easy to imagine that people are seeing ghosts simply because they expect to. This theory breaks down, however, when you consider the numerous accounts that have allegedly involved actual physical contact with a PH.

Across Archer Avenue from Chicago's Resurrection Cemetery is an old tavern called Chet's Melody Lounge. The owners have encouraged the telling of the local tale for many generations. In fact, for years the bartenders left a nightly Bloody Mary cocktail at the end of the bar for the elusive phantom, "just in case she was thirsty." And a local favorite, "The Ballad of Resurrection Mary," was a longtime offering on the bar's jukebox. Chet's enjoys a unique place in the Resurrection Mary story because numerous witnesses have come into the bar claiming that they have run her over with their car. The encounter follows the same plot line almost without deviation. A man is driving along Archer Avenue around one o'clock in the morning. From out of nowhere, as he passes the stretch of Resurrection Cemetery, a woman appears in the head-lights of his vehicle. He slams on the brakes to avoid striking her, but he's too late. In each eyewitness account, the driver testifies that he felt the vehicle make contact with the woman's body as he ran her over. Nonetheless, when he gets out to attend to the victim, she is nowhere to be found. Chet's first became associated with the legend because of the sheer number of drivers who rushed into the bar begging for help after these bizarre experiences.

Researcher Sean Tudor, in a 1997 article for *Fortean Times*, ex-plored the phenomenon of the so-called road ghost as he exam-ined the infamous phantom of Blue Bell Hill—a woman in a white dress who has occasionally been seen along a desolate British by-way in Kent since the 1960s. As Tudor states at the outset of his analysis, "it is to folklore that we must turn to gain any kind of un-derstanding of what is really happening [in such cases]." He points out that in such narratives, the witnesses, their listeners, or both almost always tie their road ghost to an historical incident along the road in question; most commonly, it is an accident involving a young woman. In the case of the phantom of Blue Bell Hill, true believers link the encounters to a real car crash in 1965 that killed a young bride just hours before her wedding.

For Chicago's Mary, there are plenty of historical antecedents to choose from. Most researchers have long believed that, in life, Mary was actually Mary Bregovy, a Polish-Czech factory worker who lived in the Back of the Yards neighborhood near the Union Stockyards. On a fateful night in the spring of 1934, on the way home from a night of dancing, she went through the window of her escort's car when the vehicle struck a support beam of the el-evated rail tracks on Lake Street. Other researchers trace the story to the 1940s, when a young Polish girl crashed near Resurrection Cemetery at around 1:20 a.m. after she took the family car to visit her boyfriend in Willow Springs. According to this version, the girl was buried in a term grave at Resurrection. A term grave is a grave that is rented out for a period of less than 100 years. When the century is up, if no one is interested in renewing the lease, the marker is removed and the grave is considered available for a new burial. In those days, however, a term grave was usually leased for only 50 years to a poor lessee, typically during a time of economic downturn such as the Great Depression. Some believe, then, that Mary was and still is restless because of her impermanent resting place.

Others remember an accident on Archer in 1936, when a black Model A sedan collided with a wide-bed farm truck at 1:30 in the morning; both witnesses and victims were traveling home from the old O. Henry Ballroom (now the Willowbrook). Only one person survived, a girl who was badly hurt, but both men and another girl perished. Still others claim that the legend is tied to one Mary Miskowski of the south side Chicago neighborhood of Bridgeport. In this narrative, Miskowski was killed crossing the street in late October in the 1930s, on her way to a Halloween party. Newer research ties the phantom hitchhiker to a 12-year-old Lithuanian-American girl named Ona Norkus (nicknamed Marija), who was killed in an auto accident after her father took her dancing at the O. Henry as a birthday treat.

Although these local, historical ties are compelling, Tudor himself also draws attention to the subjectivity of the witnesses. Referring to Carl Jung's *Man and His Symbols*, Tudor reminds us of Jung's theory that the unconscious typically manifests itself symbolically in the dream state as a woman or a man. When a woman dreams, her unconscious mind appears as a man (*animus*), and when a man dreams, his unconscious manifests as a woman (*anima*). In light of the fact that the overwhelming majority of sightings of young and beautiful phantom females, including Resurrection Mary, are reported by men, it seems highly probable that the dreamlike state imposed by lonely late-night driving could be the culprit in so many of these cases. Haven't all of us experienced very tangible sensations during dreams, especially those of crashing or falling? Couldn't this explain the numerous reports by witnesses who think they have run over their PHs? So, it is local tradition combined with the power of the unconscious mind that makes these stories so compelling—and so common.

Though the majority of PHs could potentially be explained by this relatively simple theory, in the end it is Resurrection Mary who continues to challenge itinerant drivers, time and time again. In the mid 1970s a driver was passing Resurrection Cemetery at around 1 a.m. when his attention was caught by a flash of movement inside the gates. Slowing down, he glimpsed a young woman standing on the other side of the gates, clutching the bars. Worried that she had been locked inside after closing, he made a quick U-turn to report it to the local police across the road, who were immediately dispatched to rescue the accidental prisoner. Upon their arrival, police and caretaker found the cemetery gates deserted, but their inspection of the gates revealed a chilling spectacle: not only had two of the bars been pried apart, but the impression of a pair of delicate hands remained, seemingly burned into the metal by an incredible heat. When cemetery management saw the state of the bars, it reportedly called in officials from the Catholic Archdiocese of Chicago, which operates the cemetery. They removed the imprinted bars and whisked them away for repair, but not before scores of witnesses had viewed the bars that had been burnt by this new manifestation of Resurrection Mary.

Despite the temptation to dismiss this complex paranormal phenomenon as simply a hallucination, a projection, or an extension of local history swathed in myth, firsthand reports of eyewitnesses continue to hold up under scrutiny. And so some researchers, spurred on by more than a century of experiential accounts, have tried to find an explanation for them in the roads themselves. The concept of *ley lines* originated in Britain, where Alfred Watkins, a retired brewer, first noticed that the English countryside was covered by long tracks intersecting at various points. He termed these tracks *leys* (from *lea*, meaning "meadow"). Watkins' 1925 book on ley lines, *The Old Straight Track*, garnered quite a following upon its release and created a breed of researchers (called *ley hunters*) who began to locate and map these leys. Upon further inquiry, Watkins found that residents commonly reported paranormal activity along these roads: apparitional sightings; disembodied voices; mysterious lights; and, at the points of their intersection (*nodal points*), poltergeist activity. Observation of these nodal points led some researchers to believe that such crossroads were in fact ancient sacred sites, and that extraordinary events were occurring there and along the lines themselves. Guy Underwood, a dowser, claimed that these nodal points were actually the sites of underground springs, which seemed to create spiral-shaped patterns of some kind of force around them. He also found straight lines of this same force, which he termed *holy lines*, passing through these sites. Occult investigator Stephen Jenkins speculated that poltergeist activity and other haunting phenomena may actually take their energy from nodal points. Like-minded observers have wondered if ancient cultures harbored an awareness of these energies and used them as the sacred paths to and sites of their ritual activities.

But do ley lines exist in America? In Chicago, after the Great Fire of 1871, the city was redesigned along the much-copied grid system, which organized the metropolis on a grid of 90-degree east-west and north-south thoroughfares. A few diagonal streets from the old city were retained for ease of travel. These were all built on old Native American trails, and today they are all thought to be haunted: Milwaukee, Lincoln, Grand and—you guessed it—Archer. And in another example, in the mid-19th century, one of the most ambitious engineering projects in American history played itself out on the southwest side of Chicago: the building of the Illinois and Michigan Canal. Poorly funded from the start, the project resulted in countless deaths of the Irish-American workers who built the waterway right along Archer Avenue (the route of an old Native American trail, and later named for Colonel William Archer, head of the canal project). Starvation, thirst, disease, and infighting—all were part of the deadly legacy of this project, as are the ghosts that continue to traipse the canal's storied street.

Researcher Sean Tudor wondered if the phantom of Blue Bell Hill is tied to the tainting of an ancient culture by modern encroachment, as Resurrection Mary seems to be. He relates this local phantom to the Cailleach, an Earth mother or guardian of a sacred place that typically takes the form of a beautiful young woman. Tudor noted a marked increase in sightings of the phantom during times of environmental upheaval, especially during the construction of roads and highways. Chicago researchers, too, are mindful of the fact that the building of the Illinois and Michigan canal seemed to coincide with the start of that area's extraordinary supernatural history: during its construction, a young woman in a white dress was seen near the churchyard of St. James at Sag Bridge, itself constructed on an ancient sacred Native American site.

Though new accounts of phantom hitchhikers still hold the power to shock and distress, research into the phenomenon doesn't much interest the local residents of Blue Bell Hill or Chicago's south side, or the inhabitants of a hundred other lonely roads around the world. To locals, she is one of them—a former resident, perhaps a classmate who died in high school, perhaps someone's friend's cousin, or perhaps no one real at all, if the folklorists have their say. Yet, even those Chicagoans who dismiss Resurrection Mary as a pure fairy tale know that much of what makes their local culture, their complex history, special is wrapped up in the folds of her legendary white dress. And because of this, she is, even to nonbelievers, a priceless treasure.

The phantom hitchhiker—hypnogogic vision, Jungian dream state, cultural coping, or ghost? You decide.

Parapsychology for Ghost Hunters

By Loyd Auerbach

Since the mid-1990s, interest in ghost hunting has grown exponentially, in part because of television shows, the Internet, and the availability of affordable hand-held environmental sensors. Ghost hunting and paranormal investigation groups have been putting their own ideas out there for some time now, mainly through their Websites, but more recently through other Web-based media such as podcasts and forums. Conferences eventually popped up, though these quickly devolved into events focused on television and Internet "celebrities" talking about their experiences with ghost hunting at reportedly haunted locations. The majority of people who are involved in this pursuit often refer to themselves as being in the "paranormal field." But what's largely been missing is the actual field of science that studies the phenomenon: parapsychology. Looking at the Websites, watching some of the television shows, and listening to the podcasts of people with "experience," it's clear that there is both a misunderstanding of what parapsychology is (and isn't) and a lack of interest in what it can contribute to the activities of people within the so-called paranormal community.

It would appear that the vast majority of ghost hunters believe that parapsychologists only study extrasensory perception (ESP) and psychokinesis (PK) or work with

psychics. Because the media tends to separate ghosts and hauntings (and to some degree, poltergeists) from psychic abilities, there
is a great misconception that parapsychology has nothing to do
with such things. In fact, such phenomena are, by definition, *psychic* phenomena and therefore part of the spectrum of what parapsychologists study. More than that, ESP and PK are essential to
the various models of ghosts and poltergeists—at least, to the ones
that make sense, based on the 130 years of research we have at
our disposal. Sadly, however, the great majority of people involved
in ghost hunting today have gotten their information and training
from representations in the media and from others who obtained
their information/training from the same sources. Even the "scientific investigation" label that some teams use is based on an incomplete understanding of science and the scientific method. Using
technology does not in and of itself mean one is being scientific.

In presenting this general introduction to parapsychology, I
hope to show readers that a working knowledge of parapsychology (and to a lesser degree, its predecessor, psychical research) is
essential to investigating phenomena such as apparitions, hauntings, and poltergeists. To ignore the field and its 130-year history—
which has focused on such phenomena since its inception—is, as
the saying goes, to be doomed to repeat that history. In this case,
the result is well-meaning ghost hunters and paranormal investigators essentially spending too much of their time coming up with investigative methodologies, hypotheses, models, and theories that
repeat what the early psychical researchers already concluded
more than 100 years ago. There is much one can glean from parapsychology in terms of methods, experiments, and even tools and
technology. In fact, the use of electromagnetic field (EMF) detectors comes from parapsychologists who were first trying them out
in *their* field investigations—among them myself and Dr. Andrew
Nichols. It saddens me to see people using EMF sensors without

knowing why they were first proposed, and often without knowing how to understand the data they yield in relation to the actual situation being investigated. Again, this comes from amateurs watching investigators on television using them (myself being one of the first), but in TV segments that never explain how or why they are being used in the first place.

Are you ready to learn parapsychology for ghost hunters? If so, let's get to it!

According to the Parapsychological Association's Website's FAQ section:

> Parapsychology is the scientific and scholarly study of three kinds of unusual events (ESP, mind-matter interaction, and survival), which are associated with human experience. The existence of these phenomena suggest that the strict subjective/objective dichotomy proposed by the old paradigm...may not be quite so clear-cut as once thought. Instead, these phenomena may be part of a spectrum of what is possible, with some events and experiences occasionally falling between purely subjective and purely objective. We call such phenomena "anomalous" because they are difficult to explain within current scientific models.
>
> Parapsychology only studies those anomalies that fall into one of three general categories: ESP,...mind-matter interaction (previously known as psychokinesis), and phenomena suggestive of survival after bodily death, including near-death experiences, apparitions, and reincarnation. Most parapsychologists today expect that further research will eventually explain these anomalies in scientific terms, although it is not clear whether they can be fully understood

without significant (some might say revolutionary) expansions of the current state of scientific knowledge. Other researchers take the stance that existing scientific models of perception and memory are adequate to explain some or all parapsychological phenomena.[1]

(The Association is an international scientific gathering of parapsychologists that is recognized by the American Association for the Advancement of Science.)

In other words, parapsychology is the study of psychic, or *psi* (pronounced "sigh"), phenomena. These phenomena are actually exchanges of information between living things (mainly people, of course), or between living things and the environment, or are the result of influences of living things on the environment—all of which occur without the use of what we call the "normal" senses and do not seem to be explicable by the known physical laws of nature. (*Psi*, by the way, was the term chosen by the late Dr. J.B. Rhine to refer to these experiences because it is a fairly simple term, being the 23rd letter of the Greek alphabet and denoting an unknown. *Psi* also refers to "psyche," or the mind.)

Parapsychology as a real science (as opposed to more popular concepts of the field) has to do with connections and consciousness, or mind. Not merely content with how the mind works in general with relation to behavior or perceptions (this is the role of psychology), parapsychology wants to know if consciousness has other channels of information than the five senses, whether it can connect with the minds of others, if it can reach out and affect the world directly, and if it can survive the death of the body. It's all about consciousness, but looking at it in terms of connection, interconnectedness, and existence independent of the body. So, in short form, parapsychology is the study of paranormal events, experiences, and phenomena that involve consciousness.

The three main areas of study for parapsychologists—ESP, PK, and the survival of bodily death—came out of the initial work of the early psychical researchers, specifically the Society for Psychical Research (SPR) in Great Britain, founded in 1882, and the American Society for Psychical Research (ASPR) in the United States, founded in 1885. Both organizations had rosters filled with the major scientists of the day. It's amazing how much of their early work is now available for free through Google books or the Internet Archive (*www.archive.org*). Those early researchers conducted little in the way of laboratory studies. Instead, they were the first truly scientific ghost hunters. However, they did not limit themselves to merely looking for ghosts in haunted houses. They were more interested in the question of whether the human personality can survive the death of the body. Consequently, they looked for evidence in all possible venues, from locations that seemed to have apparitions present to séance rooms, popular in the day, where mediums ostensibly were able to communicate with spirits and vice versa. It was these early researchers who first used photography to see if they could capture a ghost on film, and who first used infrared photography—not to catch spirits in the photos, but rather to catch fraudulent mediums. They were also the ones who coined the term *ectoplasm* to describe apparent "spirit matter" that exuded from the body of a physical medium (*not* unusual effects on film, as is sometimes believed). They considered mediums as worthy of study, especially with respect to using them as intermediaries to gain access to the deceased, though the researchers also raised the question of whether the information the medium gleaned was from a deceased person or simply from the mind of someone present. In other words, as scientists they looked at different sides of the same coin, considering all possible explanations—non-paranormal and paranormal—for the phenomena. They came up with models of apparitional and haunting experiences that are still in use today

ALLEN PARK PUBLIC LIBRARY #4

in the field, because they were open to different explanations and because they saw phenomena such as telepathy and clairvoyance as part of all of the paranormal models. For some reason, most ghost hunters seem to see apparitions, hauntings, and poltergeists as completely separate from other psychic phenomena. Some express their disbelief about psychokinesis (mind over matter) while in the same sentence they talk about how ghosts are able to move objects—even though this would clearly also be a case of psychokinesis.

One of the biggest reactions I get at lectures occurs when I state that ESP and PK must by necessity be involved in experiences of apparitions and poltergeists. ESP, which includes telepathy and clairvoyance, is essentially paranormal *information transfer.* PK, or mind/matter interaction, is essentially paranormal *activity.* The survival of bodily death, which includes ghosts/apparitions, reincarnation, and near-death experiences, can be called paranormal *existence.* Consider the phenomena of ghosts for a moment (which parapsychologists and the psychical researchers before us usually called apparitions): If a ghost is defined as the consciousness, personality, or spirit of a living person existing after the death of the body, it follows that we, too, are a consciousness without a body when we are dead. Here are some questions that parapsychologists have pondered for more than 100 years, and how the early researchers first conceived of the answers, most of which still hold up under scrutiny:

Q: How do ghosts perceive without senses?

A: *They use psi processes—clairvoyance, clairaudience, and so on—to pick up information.*

Q: How do ghosts speak if they lack a voice box?

A: *Since very few people actually hear a ghost's voice, it is likely a mental projection that some witnesses are able to perceive psychically.*

As not all recorders pick up the voice at the same time, it is likely a PK effect of the ghost on the recording device.

Q: How are ghosts able to interact with us?

A: *Through a combination of telepathy (the projection of their own self image) and clairvoyance (how they perceive us).*

Q: How do ghosts move things if they lack a body?

A: *Since PK is defined as "mind over matter," and since a ghost ostensibly has a mind, the ghost moves things with PK.*

Q: How do ghosts show up on photos if they have no body to reflect light?

A: *Given our relatively complete understanding of photography and the physics of light, and given the fact that not all cameras taking pictures at the same time at the same location will pick up something, and given that there are rarely any witnesses present who also see the ghost, the best explanation is that the mind of the ghost uses PK to affect the film.*

Q: (My favorite, which I wondered about since I was very young.) How can they be wearing clothes if they lack a body?

A: *As apparitional "sightings" are actually perceptions, not visual images, the clothing is simply part of the self-image projection of the apparition. Ghosts think of themselves as being of a certain age, with a certain physical appearance and in specific clothing, and people who are able to perceive the projection see all this.*

To summarize, apparitions perceive us and the world around them with psi, tell us how we should perceive them and their intentions through psi, and physically interact with the environment (EVP, photos, and even environmental sensors) with psi.

Parapsychologists and psychical researchers have always been willing to consider various explanations for the phenomenon of ghosts, including ones derived from folklore, religion, and occult or supernatural perspectives. The early researchers compared the thousands of experiences on record and cases they had investigated against various explanations. Some fit partially or completely, some were lacking in that they were incomplete, and others made no logical sense whatsoever—even considering the fact that the early researchers knew relatively little about the physical world. I've always found it interesting that even as our understanding of physics has grown, the models of the early researchers are still the best explanations for the experiences people have—that is, unless you simply want to say that spirits have unknowable powers, or are religious or magical phenomena, in which case science can't do much with them at all.

As they were considering people's ghostly experiences as evidence for survival after death, the early researchers learned to make a distinction between true consciousness surviving death and other explanations that could be behind similar experiences. These distinctions led to the three separate phenomena of apparitions, hauntings, and poltergeists. By way of an analogy, doctors often have to deal with people experiencing the same symptoms, but who have distinctly different causes behind those symptoms. The same can be said of these phenomena. Apparitions seem to represent consciousness or personality after death, although notably there are thousands of records of apparitions of living people. People can see, hear, feel, and even smell apparitions. Hauntings (what ghost hunters often call *residual hauntings* and what psychical researchers refer to as *place memory*), can be experienced or perceived in similar fashion, but they may or may not represent deceased people or past events. What this means is that on the surface, it can be tough to tell the difference between an apparition and haunting. One is a deceased person, the other essentially a recording of a person (think: "Is it live or is it Memorex?"). The difference? Consciousness. Does the ghost behave in a self-aware manner? Is the ghost aware of, and does it directly interact with, people and surroundings? Does the ghost react to external stimuli? A person acts, interacts, and reacts. A person is (generally) aware of his or her surroundings. A recording is not.

Poltergeist cases are a different animal altogether. The term was coined centuries ago (as best our scholars can figure, in Germany around the 16th century) and means "noisy ghost"; however, psychical researchers and parapsychologists have come up with another model that explains the activity and even how to deal with it, that stands apart from apparition or haunting cases. To the frustration of many parapsychologists, the lack of awareness of the intensive work done by our predecessors in the field has been ignored (or even disdained) by a large segment of the ghost hunting community, who simply use "noisy ghost" as the explanation. After all, that's what poltergeist means, right? There are so many terms still in use today that if they were still defined as they were at their inception, they would set our understanding of the world back centuries. A new understanding of a phenomenon doesn't always change its name, even if the name doesn't exactly fit any longer.

Poltergeists are distinguished from ghost and haunting cases because they are focused on chaotic and sometimes destructive (as in breaking stuff) activity with no other physical explanation. In some apparition cases, things move and even fall, generally for a relatively identifiable reason. Apparitions are rarely chaotic, however, and other than the occasional breakage due to something falling, they are rarely destructive. People very rarely perceive ghostly figures in poltergeist cases. In apparition and haunting cases, not everyone perceives ghosts, and those who do, don't necessarily have the same experience. However, anyone looking in the right direction at a flying bowl in a poltergeist case will see it. Again, whether a ghost or a living mind moves something, it's still mind over matter, or PK. In cases of poltergeist situations, it became clear to the early researchers that the lack of ghostly sightings and experiences, the lack of any apparent spirit communication, and the chaotic nature of the events all meant that they were dealing with something quite different.

This led to an alternate theory, namely, that the unconscious mind of a living person was somehow responsible for the events. Lo and behold, by pursuing that line of reasoning, researchers found they were able to pinpoint certain individuals in cases as "agents" of the activity, and could even find stress or other emotional motivations for the chaos that related directly to those agents. Working from that premise, they found that the phenomenon could often be brought to a halt by working with the agent. In some instances, agents were able to consciously do PK in the lab (though it, like the unconsciously driven PK, seems to peter out after a short time). By proposing different hypotheses for poltergeist activity and by vigorously testing those hypotheses, researchers came up with the model that we know and use today.

In the early part of the 20th century, research on psi phenomena was pulled into the laboratory primarily in order to embrace standards that were already in place in other fields. Although studying ESP and PK in living subjects was possible in the controlled laboratory environment, the study of ghosts, hauntings, poltergeists, or any other spontaneous psychic experience was not subject to such controls. For the most part, this still holds true today. Since the 1930s and the early work of J.B. Rhine and William McDougall, parapsychologists have placed the scientific focus on such controlled studies, both to try to prove the existence of psi and to isolate certain common patterns and attributes within people who are psychic. The funding for such laboratory research, while never great, has always been greater than that for field research. Researchers such as Louisa Rhine focused quite a bit on spontaneous ESP and PK experiences, and that work was supported by the parapsychology laboratory work. The same goes for many other field researchers, whose funding was directed toward the laboratory studies, while their field investigation were supported by the other work. But if parapsychology has mainly been a laboratory-based endeavor focused on ESP and PK, what do modern parapsychologists have to offer to the field investigators looking at phenomena and experiences that, by their nature, cannot be brought into the lab?

What Ghost Hunters Can Learn From Parapsychology

In addition to learning about the models for apparitions, hauntings, and poltergeists, as well as the underlying theoretical concepts behind the phenomena and experiences, ghost hunters and paranormal investigators can learn much from the laboratory research findings on ESP and PK that have come out of the field. It is the researchers in the labs who have come up with the non-paranormal explanations that are taken for granted these days, as well as the suggested relationships between the physical environment and ghostly phenomena that originally drove the use of sensors in investigations. First and foremost, it's important to remember that we are investigating phenomena that involve human perception. With such a great focus on technology, too many ghost hunters lose sight of the human piece of the equation when without that, you really have nothing to investigate. If ghosts exist (and I believe they do), people are involved—both the dead (the ghosts) and the living (the witnesses whose stories spur the investigations). With hauntings, even though the information is seemingly "locked" in the environment or in a particular object, it is people who perceive the information and events, thereby driving the very labeling of the place or item as "haunted." With poltergeist cases, it's a living person's mind driving the PK activity.

Parapsychologists have directed their research at what being psychic—having psychic experiences and abilities—actually means. This is not only relevant if you are working with people who call themselves "psychics" or "mediums"; what's important here is that *any* witness seeing a ghost or experiencing a haunting is essentially being psychic *in the moment*. Understanding why some people are more psychic than others (due to genetics, personality variables, creativity, beliefs, and so on) can help witnesses who are in distress, and provide the investigators with additional sources of information by acting as detectors of the phenomena themselves. For example, though I won't suddenly brand a witness as psychic, I will often ask a willing witness from a previous case, whom I believe had a real apparitional or haunting experience, to come along on subsequent case. From the experimental perspective, this is to see if they can have a similar experience in a new setting. If they can, this helps validate the witness's experiences in the new case, even more than an abnormal reading on any EMF meter. *They* become the sensors or detectors, but ones you can actually communicate with! Having worked with that person in the original case, it's also easy to tell when he or she is having a genuine experience in the new case, rather than one that might be driven by expectations or wishful thinking. Finally, it gives the witnesses in the new case someone to talk to who can relate to their feelings regarding the phenomena. In this sense, parapsychology can also provide some basic understanding of the mental health issues one may need to consider during a paranormal investigation.

Parapsychologists and psychical researchers have worked with self-proclaimed psychics and mediums since the inception of the field. We've learned much about the personalities, the possibilities, and the limitations of such people, and an extraordinary amount about psychic fraud. Psychics and mediums can be useful tools in the investigator's toolbox, and if they have good people skills, they can help with the clients who are in distress (which, by the way, can include the ghosts themselves). However, parapsychologists have also learned what doesn't work with psychics and mediums and how they can sometimes get in the way of an investigation. The main thing here is that psi is people-centered, and people are your best detectors and sensors. People have the experiences that we investigate. People are innately wired for experiencing and detecting the paranormal, while technology is not.

It is true that people also misinterpret their experiences and essentially fill in the blanks with their misperceptions. And of course they can lie. However, ghost hunters seem to ignore the fact that it's possible to misinterpret or misrepresent the readings on their equipment, and use those readings to support non-supportable hypotheses. As well, some researchers will be biased against the witness's experiences unless they are seemingly corroborated by the technology. Not to mention the fact that equipment can also "lie" (pick up false readings). All of this is easy to understand if we accept the fact that none of the equipment currently being used in the field can definitively detect the "paranormal," as we simply don't know what sort of energy we are trying to detect. It would be like trying to tune into music being broadcast from a totally unknown FM radio frequency, with an AM radio. We can believe with all our hearts that the music is there and that there is source for the broadcast signal, but we'll never be able to hear it if we don't know where on the electromagnetic spectrum to look for the signal. Yes, the radio is designed to detect radio waves, but not the ones we're looking for.

Let me run through some specific research findings and theories and consider briefly how they might shed light on field investigations. Many ghost hunters have already benefited from this research—as evidenced in their use of electromagnetic field detectors or in their awareness of shifts in the Earth's magnetic field, for example—but with rare exceptions many if not most them would not be able to say where this research came from or who did it.

Geomagnetic Influence

Back in the late 1970s and early 80s, Dr. Michael Persinger, along with researchers such as Dr. Stanley Krippner, looked at how fluctuations in the local geomagnetic field might correlate to psychic experiences. It was found that there was indeed a connection between field strength and these phenomena, although that connection varied according to the type of experience. For example, people were more likely to have clairvoyant and telepathic experiences in the "lows," but precognitive and PK experiences were more likely to occur in the "highs." Apparitional experiences seemed to occur more often in the highs, as well.

That clairvoyant experiences tend to occur when there are lows in the local geomagnetic field is interesting, given that one model of hauntings suggests that the witness is psychically perceiving information that has somehow been "imprinted" on the environment. In light of the observation that hauntings seem to correlate to unusually high local magnetic fields, it may very well be that hauntings are something different than psychic experiences, as some have suggested. This is why we first began using EMF detectors, by the way—to look for a possible magnetic field correlation to the phenomena, *not* to try to detect ghosts.

Local Sidereal Time

Local Sidereal Time (LST) is measured not by the rotation of the Earth around its axis or the position of the sun in the sky, but by looking at what particular stars or constellations of stars are overhead. The Sidereal day is a few minutes shorter than our 24-hour solar days, so LST does not match up exactly with normal clock time. That means that a specific time on the sidereal clock will shift from day to day.

Looking at the detailed research data from parapsychological labs in the northern hemisphere, some studies have suggested that there's a "window" in Local Sidereal Time, occurring around 13:30 LST, that seems to correlate to an upswing in psi experiences and abilities. During this window, people in psi experiments score much higher on the tasks than at other times of day or night. This could mean that something about the Earth's position in relation to the rest of the cosmos could be affecting our psi functioning. As it happens, the LST correlation seems to support the categorization of ESP as *receptive psi*, since in effect the rise is based on the receiver's LST, even when the sender is thousands of miles away. There hasn't been a real attempt to correlate LST to hauntings and apparition cases as of yet, but this is where ghost hunters and investigators could contribute to the data, perhaps by noting the timing of people's experiences and then comparing them against Local Sidereal Time. Data also needs to be correlated for southern hemisphere research and experiences. As a point of interest, Sidereal clock programs for your computer can be found at several Websites, and there are free apps available for smart phones, as well.

RNG/REG research

Since the 1960s, parapsychologists have been conducting research on whether human beings can affect random systems. Using devices that generate random number sequences (random number generators) or random internal events in a computerized system (random event generators), researchers ask subjects to focus on a non-random outcome, which could be presented to the subjects in a variety of forms of feedback, from sound to moving displays on a computer screen. In general, the generation of the random numbers or events is based on computer algorithms checked for randomness, but on occasion, and especially in the early research, researchers have used a non-harmful radioactive source element such as cesium, which decays at a truly random rate. A subject able to affect a random system to yield a non-random output is evidence for psychokinesis, albeit what is called "micro-PK," as it occurs on a small enough scale to not be visible to the naked eye, even right down to the quantum level. During the last 15 years or so, I've heard and read pronouncements by ghost hunters—some claiming to be experts—that there is no good evidence for PK. Yet the research on micro-PK is quite extensive and quite good. (Not to mention that these same folks would often describe a ghost moving something or attacking someone, which is by definition still PK.)

The RNG/REG research can definitely be applied to ghost hunting in a number of areas. There are computer programs that will allow an investigator to see if the activity in a location changes the randomness of the system running the program. There are also stand-alone RNG or REG devices commercially available that can be brought in on an investigation. Asking an apparition to participate in such an experiment is also a good idea (I've done it myself, with great success). But unlike what you see on TV, it's better to be polite and ask for such participation, rather than to yell and challenge the ghost to "do something." The downside of using the devices in a field investigation (and, to a much lesser extent, in the lab) is the possible effect of unconscious PK from the experimenter/investigator. This is known as the *experimenter effect*.

Experimenter Effect

Parapsychologists have long been aware that the expectations of the researcher or investigator can, in fact, influence certain devices in the lab and, by extension, an entire investigation. The research on micro-PK—what has often been called human-machine interaction—indicates that certain people are able to unconsciously affect machines and electronic devices. Some have a negative effect, even to the point of breaking them, while some have a positive effect, making the device work better than it normally does. This is also possible for the person running the research. This means that just as a ghost might be able to use PK to affect a recording device (digital or analog) and create electronic voice phenomena (EVP) or some other effect, investigators might unconsciously do the same. The research definitely supports this, with nearly 50 years of experimental results, but there is little data showing that apparitions can really affect computers or recording devices, mainly because we can never be certain there's a ghost present at all. This might explain why some individuals consistently get EVP while so many others do not. A very few people are prone to unconscious PK effects, while most are not.

As an alternative explanation, it's also possible that in such instances we're dealing with something in the middle. If an investigator who is prone to EVP is working, without his or her knowledge, with apparitions present, the apparitions might in turn be working with the PK of that person, turning him or her into a sort of channel or medium. I like to call such people *techno-mediums*, as the result comes through the technology.

Mediumship Research

It is quite unfortunate that the current trend in ghost hunting is equipment focused, thanks mainly to the various TV shows whose producers find flash tech more exciting than the actual ghost stories, the experiences of the witnesses, and the potential for real drama with psychics and mediums. This trend has caused many investigators to disdain working with psychics and mediums and to apparently completely ignore both the place of mediumship in the history of ghost hunting and, more generally, psychical research and the current controlled scientific research with mediums.

A number of researchers around the world have conducted excellent research on mediums during the last few decades. But it was the work spearheaded by Dr. Gary Schwartz at the University of Arizona–Tucson (and, more currently, that of Dr. Julie Beischel at the Windbridge Institute and Dr. Emily Kelly at the University of Virginia) that has taken the research to another level of scientific rigor. Given the amount of information that a medium can glean from the person being read (called a *sitter*) merely from deduction and inference, they added more and more controls in their research. By cutting off any source of observation contamination, and by creating truly blind studies (where even the researcher doesn't know the true identity of the sitter), one narrows down the potential sources of correct information. By reviewing this research, one can find techniques to control for information contamination in case investigations—or, at the very least, understand where such contamination might come from. Even more than that, one can determine the qualities common to the best mediums and psychics in order to evaluate volunteers who want to do a bit of ghost hunting. Most importantly, ghost hunters can learn how valuable such people can be in scientific research, and that working with them does not in and of itself make one's work "unscientific," as is so often asserted in the paranormal community.

Experimental Controls

Parapsychologists have learned a great deal from trial and error and from dealing with the critiques of debunkers (some relevant, some not). The lessons are clear in laboratory research: controls are needed if we are going to be able to eliminate non-psychic explanations. If we cannot do that, we cannot say with any scientific certainty that "this is psi." Again, understanding why these controls are in place in the lab can help in assessing cases for non-paranormal explanations.

Consciousness Research and Quantum Physics

During the last 15 years or so, I have seen more and more ghost hunters point to physics in order to account for the existence of ghosts. They cite parallel universes, wormholes, and other similar esoteric theories as explanations. All too often, however, these explanations don't line up with real physics or consciousness research. Not only have these explanations not been thought through to their logical conclusions, but some who put forth these models clearly don't understand where physics is in terms of what is still theoretical (for example, wormholes, parallel universes, string theory, and other dimensions) and what has been proven. One such individual with a large following on the Web has stated that physicists have proven the existence of parallel worlds when in fact they have only offered mathematical "proofs" that they *should* exist (meaning they are still theoretical). The same goes for wormholes. The reality is that physics—especially quantum physics—is both examining extraordinary and unexpected behavior and properties of particles and energy, and speculating how other such particles and manifestations of energy could possibly connect to consciousness and the effect of consciousness on the physical world. But physicists are not speculating on the existence of ghosts, nor is consciousness after death a part of their inquiry. Admittedly physics is essential to any understanding and definition of what consciousness is, but consciousness is being researched in other fields, too, including neurology and parapsychology. Parapsychologists are looking at how living consciousness affects and is affected by the world and the other consciousnesses around it, and are considering how it could exist after the death of the body (or without a body or brain to begin with), and the implications of these possibilities.

Parapsychology can point ghost hunters to the appropriate work in numerous fields, and to the work of many looking at the actual question of what consciousness is. If consciousness is merely a trick of the brain, our approach to ghosts would have to change, such that ghosts would then be a combination of projections of the living mind and information in the environment (hauntings). Such an approach is taken to heart by some parapsychologists as the best explanation available right now. Others believe that consciousness is much more than just the brain and can exist on its own. Investigators can approach a given case from either perspective, but should always consider all alternatives. Ultimately, understanding what consciousness research is and is not will help researchers assess data and help them understand that science is not in a place to state unequivocally that it has proof of consciousness. Ergo, any statements of proof about ghosts are incredibly premature and are themselves unscientific.

Alternative Non-Psychic Explanations

Partly because of the intense focus on laboratory controls in studies of ESP and PK, and how some of those controls come from observing people in the real world and looking at their psychic experiences—whether ghosts, hauntings, poltergeists, premonitions, or some other phenomenon—parapsychologists have come up with alternative explanations that were previously unknown. In other words, the explanations that ghost hunters usually turn to come directly from parapsychological research. Both the skeptics and the paranormal community have seemingly ignored the contributions of parapsychologists to the battery of alternative explanations. More importantly, how the natural phenomena that lead to these alternative explanations affect our perceptions and lead us to conclude that we are having a paranormal experience is part of the literature of parapsychology. To be a fully versed investigator is to be aware of how the environment (low frequency sound, magnetic fields, and so on) affects people, as well as what specific perceptions correlate to each of these contributing factors. Understanding things like sleep paralysis and perceptual processes can help the investigator delve into people's experiences and provide them with a good explanation when the paranormal is not at play, or when there is a mixture of the paranormal and the non-paranormal (which is what is occurring in most cases). I could go into every one of these explanations, but that would be enough for an entire book and then some. The reader should note that this information is available in books and journals written by parapsychologists, *not* ghost hunters.

Culture, Religion, and Beliefs

Parapsychologists have done extensive research on how culture and religious beliefs affect people's perceptions of and conclusions about their ghostly experiences, and how those beliefs can bias someone to draw a conclusion that is not supported by the empirical data. More than that, beliefs can make certain types of psychic experiences more prevalent than others, both for individuals and the culture at large. Beliefs can of course also shape one's reactions to these experiences and, in some instances, shape what actually happens, such as in poltergeist cases.

Parapsychology for Ghost Hunters

Once again, I must underscore that there is no technology that has been proven to detect psychic or paranormal phenomena or anything related to consciousness "energy." Researchers have noted correlations between certain environmental conditions (which technology *can* detect) and these phenomena, but they have never been able to detect ghosts directly with any of these methods. The rise of spirit communication boxes is interesting. If the boxes work as is stated—as random scanners of radio signals or localized EM fields, or simply as random event generators—then it naturally begs the question of *who* is affecting the output (the non-randomness): a ghost, or the unconscious mind of the operator? Again, because living people can affect such devices unconsciously, we'd have a hard time citing an apparitional cause unless there were some corroboration that there is indeed a ghost present. Even then, we couldn't be sure. With this in mind, the most important lesson parapsychology can teach us about the use of technology in investigations is the importance of correlating data between the technology and the actual experiences. Ultimately, it is by delving into the history of the field of parapsychology, and understanding how the scientific method has been applied in the laboratory and in field investigations, that ghost hunters can take the necessary steps themselves toward engaging in real scientific research and thus contribute to the quest for understanding of these phenomena.

Finally, it is incredibly disconcerting to see the very same people continuously asserting that there needs to be cohesiveness and cooperation to the paranormal field, trashing the work of others. Groups become territorial about their areas; they form teams with logos and t-shirts and vehicle signs, and make being in the "right" group more important than the actual investigations (and certainly more important than the clients). Many of us looking at this see it as gang behavior, with all its territoriality, "colors," and competition for cases rather than cooperation. People are also incredibly emotionally invested in their "explanations" and "protocols," yet the former are often co-opted from others, and the latter are nothing more than rules to control bad behavior on investigations rather than actual scientific methodology. Yes, there is competition in science in general, and a bit in parapsychology (competition for grants, for example). However, I can tell you that after 30-plus years in the field, parapsychologists generally get along with each other—even those with contentiously different positions about one of the central philosophical questions regarding our approach to ghostly phenomena: is it psi or is it survival?

Science is often about discourse, argument, and debate, and examining the evidence from different perspectives to see what explanation(s) fit in the moment—explanations that can easily change as more information becomes available about consciousness, perception, the brain, environmental effects, and the physics of the universe. By delving into discussions in journals and participating in (or at least observing) discussions amongst parapsychologists, ghost hunters can learn much about how to actually work together to get better data and then pool that data, examine it, and come to some conclusions. You may well ask how we can do this. The simple answer is to read the actual literature by scientific parapsychologists and people in and around the field, participate in activities at legitimate research and membership organizations, and seek out educational opportunities provided by those organizations and legitimate parapsychologists. Whatever you do, do not seek "certification" offered by people who know only a touch more than you do, as their knowledge is often gleaned from TV.

The field of parapsychology has a well-documented history. Thanks to the various book scanning projects, the early material is freely and easily available online. Other books and journals are widely available, as well, sometimes on the Internet. By learning the history, you will learn the evolution of the theories and models, and the philosophical and scientific positions of the field and its members today. You will avoid re-creating what's been done previously, and perhaps can build on it and further the field yourself.

Several organizations have categories of membership that allow participation, but at the very least they provide current and historical information about the phenomena, research, and investigation. Join the Society for Psychical Research (SPR), the Rhine Research Center, the Institute of Noetic Sciences, or the Windbridge Institute, to name a few. Support the Parapsychology Foundation. Even the Parapsychological Association has non-academic member categories that can help you connect with people in the field.

Finally, get educated. While no colleges offer degrees in parapsychology as of this writing, Atlantic University in Virginia Beach, Virginia, is developing an online parapsychology master's program planned for launch in 2011. However, various parapsychologists (myself included) have been offering distance learning courses for several years, and more of us in the field are providing courses for educational opportunities. Yet we find very few in the paranormal community taking advantage of these offerings. Perhaps because we don't certify anyone, the courses are not attractive enough. Or perhaps it's because the folks offering the courses are not TV stars, so there's less interest. Whatever the reason, it's quite frustrating for us to hear people speak of wanting to be "professional" and "scientific" and "serious" about their investigations, yet fail to follow through by getting some kind of scientific education. The effects of the economy are definitely involved in our low enrollments, of course, but from the parapsychological perspective, seeing people spend more money on a paranormal celebrity-based "conference" than on our courses, when they claim not to have money or time enough to even read a book or journal by actual researchers, can be quite off-putting. Speaking for myself, I am happy to answer questions from people who really are interested in the answers. So are most of my colleagues. We want to encourage people to learn more about our field and actually get involved, even if that means providing suggestions for reading and learning on their own if they truly are unable to take our courses for whatever reason.

Most of all, we want to encourage interest in science and a scientific approach to the phenomena and experiences. We want to develop the next generation of parapsychologists. But that also means pointing out the inaccuracies and inadequacies of the TV shows in how they deal with the paranormal, and how they have created a parallel—yet very separate—trajectory of investigation to that which developed during the last 130 years in parapsychology. Above all, we want people to understand that we're dealing with *subjective* paranormal experiences that often, but not always, have some apparent objective component and influence on the environment. In the end, it's all about perception and consciousness.

Science is more than mere documentation. There is something here, as evidenced by the millions of people who have all sorts of psychic and paranormal experiences. Capturing evidence is fine, but it's really clear that for mainstream science to accept the paranormal, something else has to happen. We need to know how it happens and, more importantly, *why* it happens. To quote my late friend, science and science fiction writer Martin Caidin: "It shouldn't be happening, but it *is!*"

I don't know about you, but I want to know why.

Notes

1. From *http://www.parapsych.org/articles/36/76/what_is_parapsychology.aspx*.

Index

About the Contributors

Loyd Auerbach

Loyd Auerbach, MS, director of the Office of Paranormal Investigations, has been investigating cases of apparitions, hauntings and poltergeists for more than 30 years. He has a graduate degree in parapsychology and a BA in cultural anthropology, and was recently appointed to the faculty of Atlantic University to teach online and to help develop a parapsychology MA program (scheduled to launch in fall of 2011 or winter of 2012). His latest book, coauthored with psychic Annette Martin, was *The Ghost Detectives' Guide to Haunted San Francisco* (Linden Publishing, 2011). He is the author of seven other books, including *A Paranormal Casebook: Ghost Hunting in the New Millennium* (Atriad Press, 2005); *Hauntings & Poltergeists: A Ghost Hunter's Guide* (Ronin Publishing, 2004); and *Ghost Hunting: How to Investigate the Paranormal* (Ronin, 2004). His first book, *ESP, Hauntings and Poltergeists: A Parapsychologist's Handbook* (Warner Books 1986), now out of print, was dubbed "the sacred text on ghosts" by *Newsweek* in 1996.

He is an adjunct professor at JFK University and teaches parapsychology at HCH Institute, both in Northern California. He's currently on the advisory boards of the Rhine Research Center, the Windbridge Institute, and the Forever Family Foundation. His media resume is impressive. He has appeared on hundreds of national and local TV shows and thousands of other venues since the early 1980s. He is also a professional mentalist and psychic entertainer, performing as "Professor Paranormal." This part of his background has made him indispensible during field investigations as well as to researchers concerned about fraud and proper controls in the lab. As of late 2009, he added the skill of professional chocolatier to his repertoire, and began selling his first chocolate products in late 2010 at *www.hauntedbychocolate.com*. Visit his Paranormal Network Website at *www.mindreader.com*.

Ursula Bielski

Ursula Bielski is the founder of Chicago Hauntings, Inc., named by Haunted America Tours as one of the top 10 ghost tours in the nation for five years running. A historian, author, and parapsychology enthusiast, she has been writing and lecturing about Chicago's supernatural folklore and the paranormal for nearly 20 years, and is recognized as a leading authority on Chicago's ghost lore and cemetery history. She is the author of seven popular and critically acclaimed books on the same subjects, including the *Chicago Haunts* series.

Ursula's interests in Chicago ghost hunting began at a young age. She grew up in a haunted house on Chicago's north side and received an early education in the city's history from her father, a Chicago police officer, who introduced Ursula to the ghosts at Graceland Cemetery, Montrose Point, and the old lockup at the storied Maxwell Street Police Station. Since that time, Ursula has been involved in countless investigations of haunted sites in and around Chicago, including such notorious locales as Wrigley Field, the Congress Plaza Hotel, Dillinger's Alley, and the site of the St. Valentine's Day Massacre. Her paranormal travels have also led to places as diverse and infamous as the Bell Witch Cave in

Tennessee; the Oshkosh, Wisconsin Opera House; the House of the Rising Sun in New Orleans; the City Cemetery in Key West, Florida; and the Civil War battlefield at Gettysburg, Pennsylvania. Ursula has been featured on numerous television documentaries, including productions by the A&E Network, the History Channel, the Learning Channel, the Travel Channel, and PBS, and as a paranormal expert on the *Maury Show*. She also appears regularly on Chicago television and radio, and in lectures throughout the year at various libraries and historical and professional societies. In addition to her books, Ursula is the author of numerous scholarly articles exploring the links between history and the paranormal, including several articles published in the *International Journal of Parapsychology*. Ursula is a past editor of *PA News*, the quarterly newsletter of the Parapsychological Association; a past president and board member of the Pi Gamma Chapter of Phi Alpha Theta, the national history honor society; and a member of the Society of Midland Authors. Ursula holds a BA degree in history from Benedictine University and an MA in American cultural and intellectual history from Northeastern Illinois University. Her academic explorations include the Spiritualist movement of the 19th century and its transformation into psychical research and parapsychology, and the relationships between belief, experience, science, and religion.

Raymond Buckland

Raymond Buckland has been interested in metaphysics for more than 60 years. In the past 40 he has had more than 60 books published, both fiction and non-fiction, with nearly two million copies in print and translated into 17 foreign languages. He has received awards for his work and been featured in several national book clubs. He has served as technical director for movies, working with Orson Wells, John Carradine, Vincent Price, and William

Friedkin (director of *The Exorcist*). He has lectured at colleges and universities across the country and been the subject of articles in such newspapers and magazines as the *New York Times*, the *Los Angeles Times*, the *New York Daily News*, the *New York Sunday News*, the *National Observer*, the *Cleveland Plain Dealer*, *Look Magazine*, *Cosmopolitan*, *True*, and many others.

Raymond has appeared on numerous national television and radio talk shows, including *The Dick Cavett Show*, *The Tomorrow Show* (with Tom Snyder), *Not For Women Only* (with Barbara Walters), *The Virginia Graham Show*, *The Dennis Wholey Show*, *The Sally Jessy Raphael Show*, and has been seen on BBC-TV, RAI-TV in Italy, and CBC-TV in Canada. He has appeared extensively on stage in England and played small character parts in movies in America. He has taught courses at colleges and universities and been a featured speaker at conferences and workshops. He is listed in a number of reference works, including *Contemporary Authors* and *Who's Who In America*.

Raymond teaches workshops at Spiritualist communities. He lives on a small farm in north-central Ohio with his wife and two Chihuahuas.

Dr. Bob Curran

Dr. Bob Curran was born in a remote area of County Down, Northern Ireland. After leaving school, he worked in a number of jobs, including gravedigger, hospital orderly, civil servant, and journalist. He travelled extensively to a number of countries before returning to Northern Ireland and entering university. Graduating with a degree in history and a doctorate in educational psychology, he has since worked in community education and rebuilding communities in the province. He currently works on a number of projects for the Office of the First and Deputy First Minister of Northern Ireland, and sits on a number of consultative bodies advising on culture. He has written widely, mainly on folklore and topics such as werewolves, zombies, vampires, and witchcraft. Dr. Bob Curran is also well-known in many parts of the world as a broadcaster and radio guest. As a former scriptwriter for comic books, he is currently working on a number of graphics projects which are in various stages of completion. He lives in Northern Ireland with his wife and family.

Larry Flaxman and Marie D. Jones

Larry Flaxman has been actively involved in paranormal research and hands-on field investigation for more than 13 years. He melds his technical, scientific, and investigative backgrounds together in pursuit of no-nonsense, scientifically objective explanations for anomalous phenomena. He is the president and senior researcher of ARPAST, the Arkansas Paranormal and Anomalous Studies Team, which he founded in February of 2007. Under his leadership, ARPAST has become one of the nation's largest and most active paranormal research organizations, with more than 150 members worldwide. ARPAST is also a proud member of the TAPS family (the Atlantic Paranormal Society). Widely respected for his expertise on the proper use of equipment and techniques for conducting a solid investigation, Larry also serves as technical advisor to several paranormal research groups throughout the country.

Larry has appeared on the Discovery Channel's *Ghost Lab* and has been interviewed for *The Anomalist*, the *Times Herald News*, the *Jacksonville Patriot*, *ParaWeb*, the *Current Affairs Herald*, and *Unexplained* magazine. He has appeared on hundreds of radio programs, including *Coast to Coast AM*, *TAPS Family Radio*, *Encounters Radio*, *Higher Dimensions*, *X-Zone*, *Ghostly Talk*, *Eerie Radio*, *Crossroads Paranormal*, *World of the Unexplained*, and *Haunted Voices*. Larry is a staff writer for *Intrepid Magazine*, and his work has appeared regularly in *TAPS ParaMagazine*, *New Dawn*, and *Phenomena*. He is also a screenwriter and popular public speaker, lecturing widely at paranormal and metaphysical conferences and events all over the country.

Marie D. Jones is the best-selling author of *2013: End of Days or a New Beginning? Envisioning the World After the Events of 2012* and *11:11: The Time Prompt Phenomenon: The Meaning Behind Mysterious Signs, Sequences and Synchronicities* (with Larry Flaxman). She is also the coauthor of *The Resonance Key: Exploring the Links Between Vibration, Consciousness and the Zero Point Grid*; *The Déjà vu Enigma: A Journey Through the Anomalies of Mind, Memory, and Time*; and *The Trinity Secret: The Power of Three and the Code of Creation*—all with Larry Flaxman, her partner in ParaExplorers.com, an organization devoted to exploring unsolved mysteries.

Marie has been interviewed on more than 100 radio talk shows, including *Coast to Coast AM*, *NPR*, *KPBS Radio*, *Dreamland* (which she co-hosts), *X-Zone*, the *Kevin Smith Show*, *Paranormal Podcast*, *Cut to the Chase*, *Feet 2 the Fire*, *World of the Unexplained*, and the *Shirley MacLaine Show*, and has been featured in dozens of newspapers, magazines, and online publications all over the world. She is a staff writer for *Intrepid Magazine*, and her essays and articles have appeared in *TAPS ParaMagazine*, *New Dawn*, *Whole Life Times*, *Light Connection*, *Vision*, *Beyond Reality*, and several popular anthologies such as the *Chicken Soup* series. She has lectured at major paranormal, new science, and self-empowerment events and is a popular public speaker. She worked as a field investigator for MUFON (Mutual UFO Network) in Los Angeles and San Diego in the 1980s and 90s, and co-founded MUFON North County. She currently serves as a consultant and director of special projects for ARPAST, the Arkansas Paranormal and Anomalous Studies Team. Marie is also a licensed New Thought/metaphysics minister.

Micah A. Hanks

Micah A. Hanks is a full-time journalist, radio personality, author, and investigator of the unexplained. He has been featured as a guest on many television and radio programs, including the History Channel's *Guts and Bolts*, the Travel Channel's *Weird Travels*, CNN Radio, and the *Jeff Rense Program*. He is also a regular contributor to *UFO Magazine*, which features his column, "Mirror Images," in each issue. You can read the latest news about UFOs and unexplained phenomena, as well as find out more about Micah's ongoing projects and appearances, on his Website, The Gralien Report (*www.gralienreport.com*), or by contacting him directly at info@gralienreport.com.

Andrew Nichols

Andrew Nichols is a psychologist, parapsychologist, hypnotherapist, and investigator of alleged poltergeist cases and other paranormal phenomena. He is a member of the American Psychological Association, the Parapsychological Association, and the Society for Psychological Hypnosis. He has been a psychology professor for many years at several north Florida colleges, and currently teaches parapsychology at Santa Fe College in Gainesville, Florida.

During his 30-year career, Dr. Nichols has investigated several hundred reported cases of ghosts, hauntings, and poltergeists, and conducted studies in telepathy, precognition, and paranormal dream experiences. He has written numerous articles on psychic phenomena for popular magazines such as *Fate*, and his scientific papers on the paranormal have been published in several respected journals such as the *Journal of Parapsychology*, the *International Journal of Parapsychology*, the *European Journal of Parapsychology*, and *Proceedings of the Parapsychological Association*.

Professor Nichols has lectured and given workshops on parapsychology at colleges and conferences throughout the United States, Canada, and Europe. He is the author of the book *Ghost Detective: Adventures of a Parapsychologist*, and his work has been featured in many books on paranormal topics. As a media consultant on the paranormal, Nichols has appeared on numerous TV and radio programs throughout the world, including *Unsolved Mysteries*, *48 Hours*, and NBC's *The Other Side*. Several television specials have featured Dr. Nichols' work, including ABC's *The World's Scariest Ghosts*, the Discovery Channel's *Real Ghosthunters* and *Ghost Detectives*, and A&E's *Beyond Death*. He has investigated alleged poltergeist disturbances for government agencies and law enforcement, including the United States Army, Oak Ridge National Laboratory, and the Daytona Beach Police Department. Dr. Nichols currently resides in Gainesville, Florida, where he maintains a private consulting practice.

Nick Redfern

Nick Redfern works full time as an author, lecturer, ghostwriter, and freelance journalist. He has written about a wide range of unsolved mysteries, including Bigfoot, UFOs, the Loch Ness monster, alien encounters, werewolves, psychic phenomena, chupacabras, ghosts, the Men in Black (MIB), and government conspiracies. He has written for Britain's *Daily Express* and *People* newspapers and *Penthouse* magazine, and writes regularly for the newsstand publications *UFO Magazine*, *Fate*, *TAPS ParaMagazine*, and *Fortean Times*. His many previous books include *The NASA Conspiracies*; *Contactees*; *Memoirs of a Monster Hunter*; *There's Something in the Woods*; and *Strange Secrets*. Nick Redfern's next book, *The Real Men in Black*, will be published by New Page Books in the summer of 2011. Nick has appeared on numerous television shows, including VH1's *Legend Hunters*; the BBC's *Out of this World*; the

History Channel's *Monster Quest* and *UFO Hunters*; the National Geographic Channel's *Paranatural*; and the SyFy Channel's *Proof Positive*. Redfern is the co-host, with Raven Meindel, of the popular weekly radio show *Exploring All Realms*. Originally from England, Nick Redfern lives in Arlington, Texas, with his wife, Dana. He can be contacted through his Website, Nickredfern.com.

Michael Tymn

A 1958 graduate of the School of Journalism at San Jose State University, Michael Tymn has contributed more than 1,500 articles to more than 40 newspapers, magazines, journals, and books during the past 53 years. Although most of his articles have dealt with subjects from the sports arena, he has also written business, travel, metaphysical, and human interest features. He won the 1999 Robert H. Ashby Memorial Award given by the Academy of Religion and Psychical Research for his essay, "Dying, Death, and After Death." His metaphysical articles have appeared in *FATE*, *Mysteries*, *Atlantis Rising*, *Vital Signs*, *Venture Inward*, *Nexus*, *Christian Parapsychologist*, *Two Worlds*, *Dark Lore*, *Psychic News*, *Alternatives*, and *Alternate Perceptions* magazines, as well as in the *Honolulu Advertiser*. Writing assignments have taken him to such diverse climes as Bangkok, Panama, Glastonbury, Jerusalem, Hollywood, St. Paul, and Tombstone.

A native of Alameda, California, Michael now lives in Kailua, Hawaii, with his wife, Gina. Since retiring from the insurance business in 2002, he has authored three books: *The Articulate Dead*, *Running on Third Wind*, and *The Afterlife Revealed*. He currently serves as vice president of the Academy of Spirituality and Paranormal Studies, and is editor of one of the organization's two publications, *The Searchlight*.

Joshua P. Warren

Joshua P. Warren is the author of a dozen books, including *How to Hunt Ghosts*, *Pet Ghosts*, *Haunted Asheville*, and *The Secret Wisdom of Kukulkan*. He hosts the *Speaking of Strange* radio program and has appeared on the National Geographic Channel, the History Channel, the Discovery Channel, Animal Planet, Sy-Fy, TLC, and many others. Numerous popular tours, based on his work, run regularly in his hometown of Asheville, North Carolina. As the founder and president of L.E.M.U.R., he and his team continue to explore the world's greatest mysteries and adapt them to practical research projects. Stay informed on new developments through his free e-newsletter, available at *www.joshuapwarren.com*.

Also Available From NEW PAGE BOOKS

Encyclopedia of Haunted Places
Edited by Jeff Belanger
EAN 978-1-60163-082-7

Lore of the Ghost
Brian Haughton
EAN 978-1-60163-024-7

Man-Made Monsters
Dr. Bob Curran
EAN 978-1-60163-136-7

The Poltergeist Phenomenon
Michael Clarkson
EAN 978-1-60163-147-9

There's Something Under the Bed!
Ursula Bielski

EAN 978-1-60163-134-3

Pet Ghosts
Joshaua P. Warren
EAN 978-1-56414-888-9

The Real Men In Black
Nick Redfern
EAN 978-1-60163-157-2

Visit NewPageBooks.com for more info or
NewPageBooks.blogspot.com for the latest news.

Searching For Answers...

Exposed, Uncovered, and Declassified: UFOs & Aliens

Featuring Original Essays by Stanton T. Friedman, Erich von Daniken, Nick Pope, Kathleen Marden, Nick Redfern, Thomas J. Carey, Donald R. Schmitt, Marie Jones & Larry Flaxman, John White,, Jim Moroney, Gordon Chism, and Micah Hanks
EAN 978-1-60163-174-9

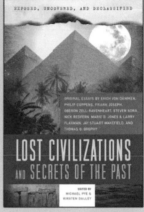

Coming in December
Exposed, Uncovered, and Declassified: Lost Civilizations & Secrets of the Past

Featuring Original Essays by Erich von Daniken, Philip Coppens, Frank Joseph, Oberon Zell-Ravenheart, Steven Sora, Nick Redfern, Marie D. Jones & Larry Flaxman, Adrian Gilbert, Paul von Ward, and Thomas G. Brophy

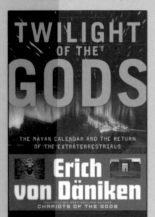

Twilight of the Gods

The Mayan Calendar and the Return of the Extraterrestrials
Erich von Daniken
EAN 978-1-60163-141-1
Includes 8-Page-Color Insert

The World's Creepiest Places
Dr. Bob Curran
Illustrated by Ian Daniels
EAN 978-1-60163-190-9

Visit NewPageBooks.com for more info.
Available Wherever Books Are Sold